THE OPEN UNIVERSITY

A Second Level Course

SOLIDS, LIQUIDS AND GASES

7 Perfect Solids
8 Thermal Properties of Solids

Prepared by a Course Team from
the Faculties of Science and Technology

The Open University Press

THE ST28- COURSE TEAM

Chairman and General Editor

R. A. Ross

Co-Chairman*

P. M. Clark

Unit Authors

P. M. Clark
C. J. Harding
B. W. Jones
I. Lowe
M. J. Pentz
R. A. Ross
M. Shott
A. J. Walton
G. Weaver

Editors

F. Aprahamian *(Faculty Editor)*
M. Harris *(Editorial Course Assistant)*

Other Members

A. V. Baez
W. A. Cooper
A. Crispin *(Staff Tutor)*
R. H. Eardley *(Research Assistant)*
R. D. Harrison *(IET)*
D. S. Jackson *(BBC)*
A. B. Jolly *(BBC)*
A. Millington *(BBC)*
P. A. B. Murdoch *(Staff Tutor)*
R. A. Shotton *(Course Assistant)*
E. Smith *(BBC)*
B. G. Whatley *(BBC)*

* Responsible for Units 11-16 (ST285)

The Open University Press,
Walton Hall, Bletchley, Bucks.

First published 1973
Copyright © 1973 The Open University

All rights reserved. No part of this work may be reproduced in any form, by mimeograph or any other means, without permission in writing from the publishers.

Designed by the Media Development Group of the Open University.

Printed in Great Britain by
Martin Cadbury Printing Group, Cheltenham and London.

ISBN 0 335 04044 6

This text forms part of the correspondence element of an Open University Second Level Course. The complete list of units in the course is given at the end of this text.

For general availability of supporting material referred to in this text, please write to the Director of Marketing, The Open University, Walton Hall, Bletchley, Bucks.

Further information on Open University courses may be obtained from the Admissions Office, The Open University, P.O. Box 48, Bletchley, Bucks.

1.1

Unit 7 Perfect Solids

Contents

Table A

List of scientific terms, concepts and principles used in Unit 7

Taken as prerequisites			Introduced in this Unit	
1 Assumed from general knowledge	2 Defined in a previous Unit	Unit No.	3 Defined and developed in this Unit	Page No.
atom		**ST28-**	perfect solid	7
ion	Newton's second law of motion	1	hexagonal close-packed structure	9
metal	force as derivative of potential	2	face-centred cubic structure	9
covalent	pair-potential function	2	body-centred cubic structure	12
energy	Lennard-Jones equation	2	surface energy	
isotropic	van der Waals interaction	2	Madelung sum	15
	Coulomb interaction	2	elastic deformation*	19
	latent heat	2	plastic deformation*	
	perfect gas	3	stress*	20
	temperature	3	strain*	20
	mechanical properties of a spring	1	Young modulus*	21
	Periodic Table	S100/9 T100/19	shear modulus	22
			bulk modulus	22
			Poisson ratio	22
			resolved shear stress	22
			fracture strength*	27
			Morse potential function	28
			Griffith criterion*	32
			stress concentration*	33
			critical shear stress	
			crystal twinning	37
			dislocation*	38
			substrate potential	39
			width of dislocation	40

* Terms thus marked will be familiar to students who have read T100 (see footnote on p. 5).

Aims

In this Unit, we try to use pair-potential functions to predict the properties of solids. To attempt this requires that we know the relative positions of atoms and this is used to define a 'perfect' solid. Predicted values of mechanical properties are compared with experimental values and, where the models show serious discrepancies, some more refined models are explored. These show the limitations of attempts to use pair potential functions.

Objectives

1 Understand and/or be capable of using in correct context the new words/phrases/concepts listed in Table A.

2 Define a 'perfect' solid. (SAQ 1)

3 Describe (using diagrams) the face-centred-cubic and hexagonal close-packed crystal structures. (Home Experiment)

4 Be able to calculate interatomic distances in simple crystals and hence, given a pair potential function, to calculate a crystal binding energy for an atom. (SAQs 2 and 3)

5 Relate the potential well depth of the pair potential function to the latent heat of sublimation and to the surface energy of a substance. (SAQ 4)

6 Outline the argument by which an expression for the bulk modulus of any solid may be derived. (SAQs 5, 6 and 7)

7 Prove that the elastic strain energy in a crystal is $\sigma^2/2E$ and deduce the expression $\sigma_f = \sqrt{E\gamma/a}$ for the fracture stress of a solid. (SAQs 7 and 8)

8 Explain the role of cracks in determining the actual fracture stress of brittle solids. (SAQ 9)

9 Calculate the shear stress component in a plane at any specified angle to an applied tensile stress. (SAQ 10)

10 Derive an expression for the maximum shear stress which a perfect solid can withstand and explain why real solids cannot support such a stress. Explain why pair potential functions are not used to calculate the shear stress needed to move a dislocation. (SAQs 11 and 12)

Study Guide

At first sight this Unit may seem a bit on the long side, but much of it is not very demanding so you should try to study it all. If you do need to do less than this optimum, however, the following strategies are recommended:

1 Do *not* omit the Home Experiment.

2 If you have previously studied S100* but not T100**, make sure you study Sections 7.7 and 7.8.

3 If you have previously studied T100 but not S100, make sure you study Section 7.6. You should find much of Sections 7.7 and 7.8 familiar.

Some of the more algebraic sections are covered by SAQs 5 and 8, which are intended to show you how to study such material. You are not expected to be able to reproduce these algebraic arguments in detail, but should be aware of the route the arguments take.

The Home Experiment is placed early in the Unit and a familiarity with its results is presumed throughout the rest of the Unit. It is therefore rather important that you should do it at the recommended place in your programme of study.

SAQs are placed in text at the point where you should be able to do them. They have been designed not only so that you should be able to check whether you have understood what you have just studied, but also so that you can use them for revision, i.e. you can do them more than once. So don't save them for October, please!

* The Open University (1971) *S100 Science: A Foundation Course*, The Open University Press.

** The Open University (1972) *T100 The Man-made World: A Foundation Course*, The Open University Press.

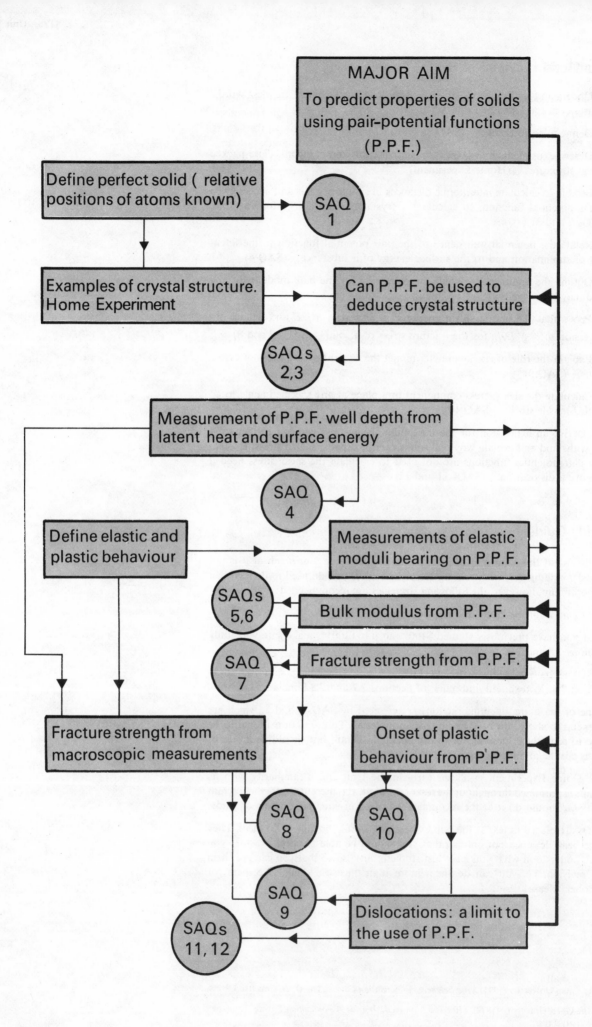

MAJOR AIM
To predict properties of solids using pair-potential functions (P.P.F.)

Define perfect solid (relative positions of atoms known)

SAQ 1

Examples of crystal structure. Home Experiment

Can P.P.F. be used to deduce crystal structure

SAQs 2,3

Measurement of P.P.F. well depth from latent heat and surface energy

SAQ 4

Define elastic and plastic behaviour

Measurements of elastic moduli bearing on P.P.F.

SAQs 5,6

Bulk modulus from P.P.F.

SAQ 7

Fracture strength from P.P.F.

Fracture strength from macroscopic measurements

Onset of plastic behaviour from P.P.F.

SAQ 8

SAQ 10

SAQ 9

Dislocations: a limit to the use of P.P.F.

SAQs 11, 12

7.1 Introduction: What is a 'perfect' solid?

In Unit 2 we looked at the effect of competing kinetic and potential energies in an atomic system. The potential energy of the atoms was, you will remember, due to the existence of forces between the atoms. We saw that when the kinetic energy of the atoms ($\frac{3}{2}$ kT on average) was very much greater than the potential energy we expect the system to exist as a gas. We then chose to presume a system in which the potential energy of every atom was always zero, and this defined a perfect gas. On the other hand we saw that if the kinetic energy was very much less than the potential energy we would expect the matter to exist as a solid. We are now going to consider a model in which the molecular kinetic energy is presumed identically equal to zero and let this define a perfect solid. At least, this is half the definition of a perfect solid; for reasons of simplicity it is a good idea to postulate also that the atoms of the solid should be regularly arranged in space. This restricts the application of the model to crystalline solids, which, as you will see in the TV programme, do possess a regular repetitive atomic structure. The extra postulate excludes glasses, in which the atomic arrangements possess no long-range orderliness.

For the perfect solid so defined, we can in principle write down an expression for the potential energy of an atom within the bulk of the solid by adding together the potential energies of interaction of that atom with every other atom in the solid.

By now you know enough about interatomic forces to be able to write down what information is necessary to enable such a sum to be done.

What information is needed?

These two points are different in kind. The first point specifies the atomic geometry of the solid, whereas the second enables the potential energy of a particular pair to be calculated. However, the nature of the interatomic forces is an important factor determining the crystal geometry, so in reality the items mingle.

What possibly dangerous assumption has been made?

---

1 The distance of every atom from the chosen one.

2 The interatomic potential function for a pair of atoms.

That the interatomic forces are independent of intervening atoms between members of a pair.

Unit 2 also briefly reviewed the classification of forces between atoms; van der Waals forces, Coulomb forces between ions, the covalent and metallic bonds. Now it is fortunate for the purposes of this Unit that we can select solids in which only one of the attractive interactions is dominant. There are some solids in which the only attractive forces between atoms are the weak van der Waals interactions: the inert (or 'noble') gas elements. Then again other solids are built of molecular rather than atomic units. The molecules are built up of covalently bonded atoms but only van der Waals forces act *between* the molecules; nitrogen (N_2 molecules) and methane (CH_4 molecules) are examples. You will notice that these two examples are also gases down to low temperatures, which means that $\frac{3}{2}$ kT exceeds the intermolecular potential energy when T is small, which in turn suggests that the forces between the molecules are very weak.

There are van der Waals attractive forces between all atoms, but when there are also ionic or covalent or metallic bonds the much weaker van der Waals inter-actions can safely be ignored in all but the most rigorous work (which this Unit is not). It is only simple to establish a pair-potential function for systems in which only one of the three types of chemical bond is present. Thus diamond is a supreme example of covalency without any possibility of ionic bonding and sodium chloride is the archetypal ionic compound. We shall refrain from con-sidering substances in which the bonding is intermediate between the two extremes. Metals are easily identified, but as we shall see the metallic bond presents its own peculiar difficulties of interpretation in terms of a pair-potential function.

In this Unit we shall assume that in a perfect solid we know where the atoms are and that there is one dominant attractive force acting between them. From this we shall predict various measurable properties of solids. We can test these predictions against experiment. Sometimes we shall 'succeed', that is we shall find agreement between our predictions and our experiments—other times we shall 'fail', that is we shall show the model to be inadequate to explain those phenomena. Unlike the perfect gas theory (in which discrepancies of a few per cent between theory and experiment may be regarded as failures), when the perfect-solid model fails, it can do so by several orders of magnitude. Among the properties explored in this Unit are some mechanical properties of crystals: their bulk modulus, their shear strength and their tensile strength. These properties are particularly suitable for showing the range of applicability of the model and can also reveal some of the ways in which the model has to be modified to meet the demands of observation. A rather different view of 'imperfection' follows in Unit 8.

Summary

A 'perfect' solid is a solid in which the relative positions of atoms are fixed and possess a regular repeating pattern.

Such a solid cannot exist any more than can a 'perfect' gas. An approximate realization of a perfect solid is a crystal at low temperature because

1   Atoms are packed together in some *regular* pattern in crystals (see TV programme).

2   The atoms are not moving very much, so in any expression of energy of an atom the potential energy term will dominate the kinetic energy term. We might arbitrarily suggest a temperature of $0.1 \times$ melting temperature in K. Then $kT \approx 0.1 \times$ potential energy.

> SAQ 1   Identify items from the following list which adequately define a 'perfect' solid.
>
> 1   Matter in which atomic kinetic energy is much less than atomic potential energy.
>
> 2   Matter in which atoms are arranged in a regular array.
>
> 3   A crystal at low temperature.
>
> 4   A glass at low temperature.
>
> 5   Matter in which atomic kinetic energy is zero.
>
> 6   A crystal just below its melting temperature.

7.2   Some simple packing patterns for atoms

For this Section and the next, you will need Home Kit items 18, 43 and 61. Also you will need your tape recorder and cassette number 3 and about one hour of time.

Can you think of three factors which could influence how atoms pack together?

1   Their size.
2   Their shape.
3   The nature of the forces between them.

Can you suggest the simplest combination of these factors for us to examine?

1   Let us have all the atoms the same size.
2   Let us assume the atoms are spherical.
3   Let us assume isotropic attractive forces between atoms whose centres are further apart than one atomic diameter (D) and an infinite repulsive force for all distances less than D. (This last assumption amounts to supposing that the atoms are hard, so we won't have to worry about any change of shape due to atoms being squashed.)

How do you think equal, spherical and attractive atoms will pack?

As closely as possible; provided the atoms can juggle around, the attractive forces will keep pulling them closer together until every atom touches as many others as can be fitted around it.

In fact such 'close-packed' crystal structures are formed only by the inert gas elements and some metals. This might imply that the forces between such atoms are isotropic—but see Section 7.5.1.

Now follow the tape instructions for the Experiment.

7.3 Interactions between more than two atoms

In gases at modest pressures, say, up to one atmosphere, an atom spends most of its time so far from any other atom that the moments of interaction are regarded as collisions. At higher pressures (above ten atmospheres), the atoms are closer together and there are noticeable effects of more continuous action of interatomic forces. In solids, the atoms are packed really close together and there are always several atoms close to any given atom (say within two or three atomic diameters). Unless the attractive term in the interatomic potential function falls off very rapidly with distance, a calculation of the energy of any atom within the lattice will have to include a large number of atom-pair interactions.

> For van der Waals interactions between two atoms at distance x between centres, the attractive term in the potential energy function is proportional to $1/x^6$.
>
> Compare the potential energy of interaction of atoms at distances x, $2x$, $3x$.

At distance x put energy $E_1 = 1/x^6$
Then at distance $2x$ the energy is

$$E_2 = \frac{1}{(2x)^6} = E_1/64$$

And at distance $3x$ the energy

$$E_3 = \frac{1}{(3x)^6} = E_1/729$$

> Repeat the previous exercise for the Coulomb interaction as between ions.

We may conclude from these exercises that to ignore any interactions other than those of immediate neighbours might be justifiable for van der Waals bound atoms, but would be most unwise in calculations on ionic solids.

Let us now try to find some indications of distant atom interactions in the crystal structures of solids.

The potential energy is now proportional to $1/x$ so the relative contributions to the total potential energy for atoms at the given separations are E_1 to $E_1/2$ to $E_1/3$.

7.3.1 Distant neighbour interactions in van der Waals solids

The close-packed structures you have just discovered are shown in Figure 1.

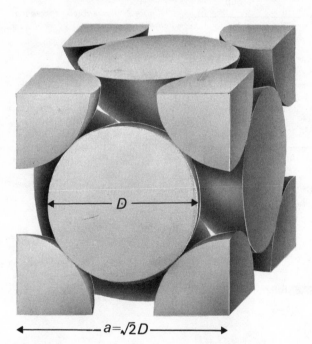
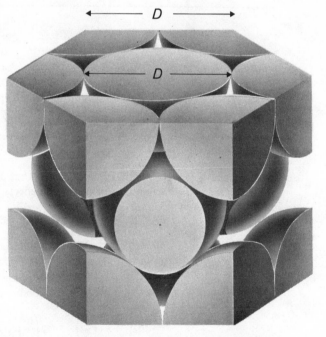

Figure 1 *Structure cells of the close-packed crystal structures: (a) face-centred cubic; (b) hexagonal close-packed.*

The atoms of the inert gas latter elements interact via van der Waals forces only and crystallize in the close-packed face-centred cubic (fcc) structure. Thus it is reasonable to suppose that the binding energy for every atom is greater if the atoms are arranged fcc than if they take up the hexagonal close-packed (hcp) structure. We have an equation for the potential energy of a pair of atoms interacting by van der Waals forces, and we know the geometries of the two structures. In principle, we can therefore calculate the binding energy of a given atom by adding together the potential energies due to its interactions with each atom in its vicinity.

Both geometries provide every atom with their twelve nearest neighbours at a distance (between nuclei) of one atomic diameter and their six next nearest neighbours at a distance of $\sqrt{2}$ (i.e. 1.414) atomic diameters. This implies that the source of preference for one geometry over the other lies with the interactions of more distant atoms, in spite of the small effects predicted in the calculation above.

The distances between atoms in these structures can be calculated using Pythagoras's theorem. In three dimensions (Fig. 2), this theorem becomes $r^2 = x^2 + y^2 + z^2$ where x, y and z are mutually perpendicular. In the fcc structure, the atoms at the corners of the cube touch those in the centres of the faces so the face diagonal is $2D$ long (D being the diameter of an atom). The edge length a of the cube is therefore found by:

$$a^2 + a^2 = (2D)^2$$
$$2a^2 = 4D^2$$
$$a = \sqrt{2}D$$

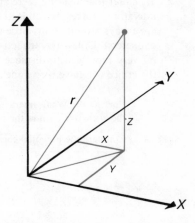

The body diagonal (l) is given by

$$l^2 = a^2 + a^2 + a^2 = 3(\sqrt{2}D)^2$$
$$\therefore l = \sqrt{6}D$$
$$= 2.45D$$

A full calculation of the numbers and positions of neighbours is tedious rather than difficult, so the results are presented (Table 1) without the working.

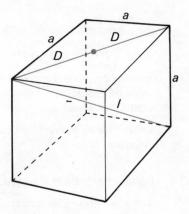

Figure 2   *Pythagoras's theorem in three dimensions.*

Table 1

Distance from given atom (in units of atomic diameter)	Number of atoms	
	fcc	hcp
1	12	12
1.414 ($\sqrt{2}$)	6	6
1.633 ($\sqrt{8/3}$)	0	2
1.732 ($\sqrt{3}$)	24	18
1.915 ($\sqrt{11/3}$)	0	12
2.000 ($\sqrt{4}$)	12	6
Total	54	56

The Lennard-Jones potential was introduced in Unit 2 (SAQ 5), and is appropriate for atoms interacting by van der Waals effects. The expression for this potential was given in Unit 2 as

$$V(r) = 4\epsilon \left\{ \left(\frac{\sigma}{r}\right)^{12} - \left(\frac{\sigma}{r}\right)^6 \right\}$$

where $\sigma = r_0/6\sqrt{2}$ (to show this was the subject of the SAQ referenced above). Substituting this value for σ into the equation produces

$$V(r) = \epsilon \left\{ \left(\frac{r_0}{r}\right)^{12} - 2\left(\frac{r_0}{r}\right)^6 \right\} \tag{1}$$

where ϵ is the depth of the potential well, and r_0 the equilibrium spacing between centres of atoms.

The energy due to the van der Waals attraction varies as $1/r^6$. The repulsive term goes as $1/r^{12}$, which is so much more rapidly changing that we need consider only repulsion between immediate neighbours and next nearest neighbours.

The potential energy of an atom in an fcc crystal is then given by

$$V_{\text{fcc}} = \epsilon \left(\frac{12}{1^{12}} - \frac{2.12}{1^6} + \frac{6}{(\sqrt{2})^{12}} - \frac{2.6}{(\sqrt{2})^6} - \frac{2.24}{(\sqrt{3})^6} - \frac{2.12}{(\sqrt{4})^6} - \dots \right)$$

$$= \epsilon (12 - 24 + 0.094 - 1.5 - 1.778 - 0.365 - \dots)$$

$$= -15.569 \, \epsilon$$

For the hcp structure, the first four terms of the series are the same, only atoms at distances greater than $\sqrt{2}r_0$ can affect the energy. The sum out to $2r_0$ is

$$= -15.625 \, \epsilon$$

Check this figure.

$$V_{\text{hcp}} = \epsilon \left\{ \frac{12}{1^{12}} - \frac{2.12}{1^6} + \frac{6}{(\sqrt{2})^{12}} - \frac{2.6}{(\sqrt{2})^6} \right.$$

$$- \frac{2.2.\sqrt{3^6}}{(\sqrt{8})^6} - \frac{2.18}{(\sqrt{3})^6} - \frac{2.12.\sqrt{3^6}}{(\sqrt{11})^6}$$

$$\left. - \frac{2.6}{(\sqrt{4})^6} - \dots \right\}$$

$$= \epsilon \{12 - 24 + 0.094 - 1.5$$

$$- 0.211 - 1.333 - 0.487$$

$$- 0.188 - \dots\}$$

$$= -15.625 \, \epsilon$$

Thus it seems that the hcp structure has the lower energy!

Well that looks wrong, doesn't it? The observed crystal structure is the one with the higher energy.

Criticize the calculation so far.

(a) The difference in energy is $0.056 \, \epsilon$, which is smaller than the last term in either series. The summation should therefore be extended to cover more atoms.

(b) We have counted 56 atoms in the hcp series, but only 54 in the fcc series.

We can correct for the difference in the number of atoms in each series by discounting two of the atoms at distance two units for the hcp series. The energies then work out to $-15.569 \, \epsilon$ for fcc and $-15.582 \, \epsilon$ for hcp. The bias in favour of hcp is then only 0.09 per cent.

If we extend the summation over larger numbers of atoms, the difference in energy between the structures stays very small. For clusters of 78 atoms there is a bias of 0.058 per cent in favour of fcc, whereas counting interactions over 174 atoms reduces this to 0.03 per cent.

Now let us appraise critically whether these small energy differences can really determine which structure will form. You have learned earlier in the Course that the depth of the potential well in which an atom in a solid rests can be estimated from latent heat measurements. In the TV programme for Unit 2 we made this estimate for argon and arrived at a figure of 1.2×10^{-20} joule/atom. The crystal will begin to form when the kinetic energy of atoms is of the same order as the depth of the potential well or a bit less; let's guess that atoms having kinetic energy of less than 0.12×10^{-20} joule (that is 1/10 of the average) are the ones which start to assemble into a crystalline cluster. The energy difference just calculated is less than 0.1 per cent of the potential well depth, i.e. less than 0.0012×10^{-20} J/atom. Our hypothesis demands, therefore, that the structure shall be sensitive to variations of potential energy of about 10^{-23} J/atom, while the kinetic energy of the atoms is at least 100 times greater than this. The statistical variation of kinetic energy is so many times greater than this that we cannot realistically expect the crystal structure to be determined by the potential energy difference that we have calculated. Indeed, what we would expect out of such a system would be a mixture of the two types of crystal to form. This is not observed.

We might bring several other doubts to bear; for example, exactly how does a crystal grow? Can a crystal structure, developed in a small cluster of atoms, change to another structure as the cluster grows? Such matters however lie beyond the model of perfect solids, depending, as they do, on the motion of atoms within solids. We have deliberately excluded motion of atoms from the model for this Unit but will consider it in the next Unit.

If we now return to the hypothesis that the fcc structure must have lower energy than the hcp structure for inert gas elements, we are forced to conclude that our

11

calculation is wrong in some fundamental way. It has failed to reveal a large enough energy difference between the two structures to account for the observed invariable appearance of fcc crystals. To maintain the hypothesis we are forced to suspect the $1/r^6$ potential function. Detailed theoretical treatments of van der Waals forces show that although $1/r^6$ is a good function for the interaction between *two* atoms, it does *not* hold for more than two atoms mutually interacting. The presence of other electrons and nuclei along the line of action of the force between a pair of atoms can drastically alter the magnitude of that interaction. The 'dangerous assumption' of Section 7.1 has proved to be unfounded here.

The lesson to be drawn is a cautionary one. If we wish to apply to solids the van der Waals force laws developed in Unit 2, we will generally have to limit discussion to interactions between nearest neighbours. By doing this we are bound to render our theoretical results inaccurate, typically by amounts around 20 per cent. 'Good agreements' between experiment and theory in this work thus implies 'in the same street' rather than 'to the nth significant figure'.

SAQ 2 Figure 3 shows a cell of the 'body-centred cubic' (bcc) crystal structure common among metals.

(a) Does this structure contain close-packed planes of atoms?
(b) Does this structure contain close-packed lines of atoms? Specify them.
(c) How many atoms are there in the cell shown?
(d) What is the edge length of the cube in atom diameters?
(e) What fraction of space is occupied by atoms (assuming them to be hard spheres)?
(f) Taking the atom at the centre of the cell as a reference, how many nearest neighbours has it got?
(g) How many next nearest neighbours has it got and how far away are they?
(h) If a van der Waals solid adopted this structure, what depth do you estimate the potential well would be?
(i) How much does this differ from the estimate for an fcc structure?
(j) Would you expect to find a solid bound by van der Waals forces to have the bcc structure?

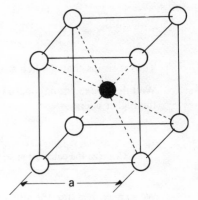

Figure 3   The body-centred cubic structure cell.

7.3.2   Distant neighbour interactions in ionic solids

As you saw in the exercise at the beginning of Section 7.3, we have most certainly got to find ways of taking into account distant-neighbour interactions for ionic solids. The electrostatic potential between ions falls off only as $1/r$ so, compared with all other interatomic interactions, the Coulomb interaction has a very long range of influence. Now, I want to discuss the effects of distant-neighbour interactions on the crystal structure of ionic solids. In Section 7.1, sodium chloride was identified as a substance in which the bonding is wholly ionic. It is also convenient in that the two types of ion, Na^+ and Cl^-, carry charges of equal magnitude (one electron unit). There are, of course, many substances for which general formulae A^+B^- can be written but, when the ionic charges are greater than one electron unit, the bonding is less than completely ionic so we will restrict our thoughts to the alkali halides* and in particular we will concentrate on sodium chloride.

In sodium chloride the ions are formed by the complete transfer of an electron from a sodium atom to a chlorine atom. Such a transfer leaves the ions with inert gas electron structures. For the positive ions, the excess charge resides on the nucleus of the atom. The extra one electron on each negative ion is somewhere in the electron cloud, but we can also assume these ions to be spheres with effectively central negative charge. We shall use this approximation in due course in an endeavour to set up an equation for the potential energy of an ion in a crystal of such a solid.

For the moment, however, let us consider qualitatively how the Coulomb forces dictate the crystal structure of simple ionic solids. You should remember that bodies carrying electric charges of like sign repel one another, whereas those carrying charges of opposite sign attract one another. It is therefore a 'safe bet' that the immediate neighbours of any ion will be ions carrying charge of opposite sign. But these neighbours will interact with one another repulsively, and we

---

* 'Alkali halide' is the general name of compounds of the 'alkali' metals of Group 1 of the Periodic Table (Li, Na, K, Rb, Cs) and 'halogens' of Group 7 (F, Cl, Br, I).

shall see that this reduces the packing density of the crystal as compared with the close-packed structures we have so far investigated.

In your Home Kit you will find a packet of small cylindrical magnets. You can use these to simulate the effect of packing charged ions. Get the magnets now and follow these instructions:

1   Put two of the magnets sides together so that their unlike poles are adjacent (the ends of the magnets are distinctively marked).

2   Now bring up a third magnet and try to form a close-packed group like this, ⁰₀⁰. You can't?

3   Bring in more magnets and attempt to surround one magnet pole with several others of opposite sign. Sketch the configuration for 3, 4, 5 and 6 magnets in the cluster.

When I did this experiment I found the patterns shown in Figure 4.

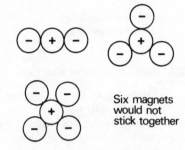

Six magnets would not stick together

Figure 4

You see that the nearest neighbour of any negative magnet pole is the positive pole at the centre of the array. The *next* nearest neighbour of any negative pole is *another* negative pole *and it is the repulsion between these poles which dictates the shape of the array.*

To carry this idea over to three-dimensional packing of oppositely charged spheres is fairly simple: every sphere of one sign will be touched (nearest neighbours) by some number of spheres of the other sign, but those spheres will arrange themselves as far apart as they can while still touching the centre sphere of the cluster. If the spheres are ions there is just one extra item to allow for; the sizes of the ions. If, say, large negative ions are to surround a small positive ion the packing is likely to be different from that with ions of similar size.

> Can you explain why this might be so?

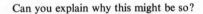

These ideas can be seen in action in the crystal structures of sodium chloride (Na^+Cl^-) and cesium chloride (Cs^+Cl^-). The radii of the ions involved are given in Table 2.

Table 2

Ion	Radius/nm
Na^+	0.098
Cs^+	0.167
Cl^-	0.181

The forces between ions of the same sign depend on distance. A large positive ion at the centre of a cluster would hold surrounding negative ions further apart than would a small positive ion.

The crystal structures of these two salts are not the same (Fig. 5), showing the importance of the different ion sizes. Eight chlorine ions can pack around the big cesium ions to give a body-centred cubic structure but only six chlorine ions can surround the smaller sodium ions, producing a face-centred cubic structure.*

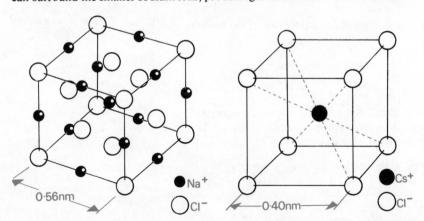

● Na^+	● Cs^+
○ Cl⁻	○ Cl⁻

0·56nm   0·40nm

Figure 5   Crystal structures of (a) sodium chloride, (b) cesium chloride.

* But *not* a *close-packed* face-centred cubic structure.

It should also be obvious that larger ions pack with greater distance between centres and in consequence the strength of the ionic bond depends upon ion size. The melting points of a series of alkali halides demonstrate this (Table 3).

Table 3

Substance	NaF	NaCl	NaBr	NaI
Ion spacing/nm	.231	.281	.294	.318
Melting point/K	1261	1074	1013	933

7.3.2.1   Calculation of the electrostatic potential energy of an ion in a crystal

Because the Coulomb force decreases so slowly with distance, a large number of ion pair interactions have to be calculated to get an accurate figure for the potential energy of an ion in the crystal. Subtle methods have been developed for reducing the labour involved, but these veil the physics of the situation so we will undertake two calculations both of which are incomplete but in different respects. First let us calculate the electrostatic potential of an ion in a sodium chloride lattice going out to the third nearest neighbours. Figure 6 shows that any ion has

6 nearest neighbours of opposite sign at distance r_0

12 next nearest neighbours of same sign at distance $\sqrt{2}\,r_0$

8 third nearest neighbours of opposite sign at distance $\sqrt{3}\,r_0$

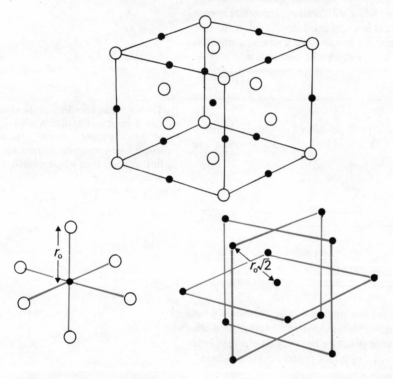
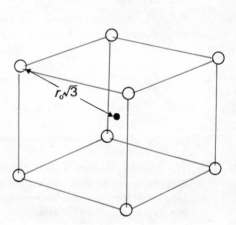

Each ion carries a charge of $+$ or $-\,e$ so the Coulomb potential of the central ion due to these 26 neighbours is

Figure 6   *Neighbours in a sodium chloride crystal.*

$$V_{\text{Coulomb}} = \frac{-e^2}{4\pi\epsilon_0 r_0}\left\{6 - \frac{12}{\sqrt{2}} + \frac{8}{\sqrt{3}}\right\} = -2.13\,\frac{e^2}{4\pi\epsilon_0 r_0}$$

This calculation is for a three-dimensional *finite* lattice out to third nearest neighbours: my other calculation is for an *infinite* one-dimensional crystal, i.e. a line of ions alternately positively and negatively charged (Fig. 7).

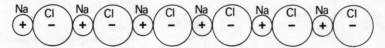

For this array the energy of any ion due to its two neighbours is $-2e^2/4\pi\epsilon_0 r_0$. The next nearest neighbours (necessarily of the same sign as the ion whose potential we are calculating) are each at distance $2r_0$ and so contribute

Figure 7   *A one-dimensional sodium chloride 'crystal'.*

14

$+2e^2/(4\pi\epsilon_0 \times 2r_0)$. Counting the ions in pairs outwards then gives us an infinite series for the potential;

$$\frac{-e^2}{4\pi\epsilon_0 r_0} \times 2\{1 - \tfrac{1}{2} + \tfrac{1}{3} - \tfrac{1}{4} + \dots\}$$

For this series, it happens to be easy to work out the sum of the whole infinite number of terms since

$$\log_e(1 + x) = x - \frac{x^2}{2} + \frac{x^3}{3} - \frac{x^4}{4} + \dots$$

Thus our series is $2\log_e(1 + 1)$ and the potential is

$$V_{\text{Coulomb}} = -(e^2/4\pi\epsilon_0 r_0) \times 2\log_e 2 = -1.38\, e^2/4\pi\epsilon_0 r_0.$$

This expression holds for any ion, whether positive or negative, anywhere in the line.

The important feature about both these calculations is that the potential for an ion among an assembly of ions is given by (constant) × (potential of a nearest neighbour pair). Thus, provided we can find the correct value for the constant (it is called the 'Madelung sum'), we can take care of the long-range Coulomb forces in ionic crystals. Working on the centralized charge approximation, the full calculation gives 1.748 as the Madelung sum for crystals of the sodium chloride structure. For the cesium chloride type structure the figure is 1.763.

SAQ 3 Work out the Madelung sum for the line of dipoles shown in Figure 8, given that the force between a pair of dipoles varies as r^{-4}.

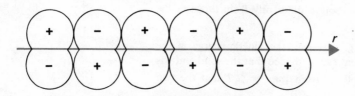

Figure 8

One interesting calculation we can now do will show how the repulsive term in the Coulomb interaction opens up the crystal structure. In the vapour phase, sodium chloride exists as NaCl molecules with interatomic spacing $r_{\text{mol}} = 0.236$ nm. This spacing results from a balance between the attractive Coulomb force between the ions and a short-range repulsive force proportional to r^{-10} (see Unit 2, Section 2.3.1). For this molecule we can write

$$V(r) = \frac{-e^2}{4\pi\epsilon_0 r} + \frac{A}{r^9} \qquad (2)$$

for its potential energy. The equilibrium spacing r_{mol} is given by $dV(r)/dr = 0$, which gives $A = e^2 r_{\text{mol}}^8/36\pi\epsilon_0$. We can use this value of A in an expression for the potential energy of a crystal of sodium chloride. The r^{-10} repulsive force falls off so quickly with distance that we need apply it only to nearest neighbours, of which every ion has six. The potential energy per ion is therefore:

$$V(r) = \frac{-e^2}{4\pi\epsilon_0}\left\{\frac{1.75}{r} - \frac{6r_{\text{mol}}^8}{9r^9}\right\} \qquad (3)$$

The minimum of this potential well occurs at $r = r_0$, where the derivative $dV(r)/dr = 0$, i.e. when the derivative of the bit in brackets is zero. Then

$$\frac{1.75}{r_0^2} = \frac{6r_{\text{mol}}^8}{r_0^{10}}$$

$$\therefore \qquad r_0^8 = 3.43\, r_{\text{mol}}^8$$

$$\text{so} \qquad r_0 = 1.17\, r_{\text{mol}}$$

But $r_{\text{mol}} = 0.236$ nm, so the spacing in the solid is 0.276 nm. The spacing calculated from X-ray diffraction measurements is 0.282 nm, so agreement is quite close. The reason for the increase of the Na–Cl distance is perhaps best seen in a diagram (Fig. 9). The ions on either side of a 'molecule' in the crystal are pulling the ions in the molecule further apart.

EXERCISE Use the Madelung sum for a line of ions and an appropriate repulsion term for nearest neighbours to calculate the spacing of Na^+ and Cl^- ions in an infinitely long line. The answer will be found on p. 16.

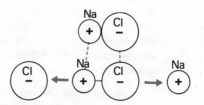

Figure 9 The effect of adjacent ions on the ion pair spacing.

7.4 Estimates of potential well depth ϵ from experimental data

7.4.1 ϵ from latent heat measurements

You have read in Unit 2 the nearest neighbour approximation relating latent heat to well depth. Let us review this argument.

To convert a solid to vapour involves separating each atom from all its neighbours. If there are N atoms in the sample and each has $\tilde{n}$ nearest neighbours there are $N\tilde{n}/2$ bonds* in the solid. The 2 comes in because each bond is between two atoms; it is the same bond that holds atom A to atom B as holds atom B to atom A. Dividing by 2, therefore, avoids counting each bond twice,

If ϵ is the depth of the potential well from which two atoms have to be lifted in order to separate them, and L_s is the latent heat of sublimation, i.e. the amount of energy needed to separate all the atoms, we have

$$L_s = \frac{N\tilde{n}\epsilon}{2} \qquad (4)$$

There are several simplifications in this argument.

1   Only bonds between nearest neighbours have been counted.

2   If the gas formed is not at zero pressure, there will still be some potential energy of binding even after evaporation.

3   Atoms at the surface of the solid are bound differently from those in the interior of the specimen.

4   The atoms of the solid are vibrating. However, the kinetic energy in the lattice will not cause any error in the latent heat provided that the solid and gas are at the same temperature. It then follows from $\frac{1}{2}m\overline{u^2} = \frac{3}{2}kT$ that the two kinetic energies are the same (Fig. 10).

Latent heat data is given for a few substances in the following table.

Table 4

Substance	Latent heat kJ mol^{-1}	ϵ/J	Energy needed to remove one electron from an atom or molecule /J
Ne	1.3	3.6×10^{-22}	3.5×10^{-18}
Ar	7.6	2.1×10^{-21}	2.5×10^{-18}
Kr	10.5	?	2.2×10^{-18}
N_2	5.9	1.6×10^{-21}	2.5×10^{-18}
CCl_4	32	8.9×10^{-21}	1.8×10^{-18}
H_2O ($\tilde{n} = 6$)	46	2.6×10^{-20}	2.0×10^{-18}

(Work out the value of ϵ for krypton for yourself.) In calculating ϵ, I have assumed $\tilde{n} = 12$ for all these substances except water. Strictly, our theory can only apply to spherical molecules since for others the orientation of one molecule with respect to another is liable to be important. N_2 and CCl_4 are not too far from spherical. H_2O certainly is not spherical and, moreover, has a non-uniform electric charge distribution which shows up as a large ϵ. The important point to notice, however, is that these intermolecular potential energies are mostly of the order 0.001 to 0.1 times the binding energies of electrons *within* molecules. This is why, for the most part, molecules maintain their integrity even as hot gases.

The binding energy of ionic solids cannot be reliably found from latent heat measurements. In the vapour phase, sodium chloride exists as ion pairs—NaCl molecules we might say. In the solid, however, no one Na^+ ion 'belongs' to any

---

* The word 'bond' is used throughout this Unit to mean any binding interaction between two atoms. This is a looser meaning than is customary among chemists, who tend to reserve the word for the result of a covalent interaction between two atoms.

ANSWER TO EXERCISE ON P. 15.

There are now two nearest neighbours and the Madelung sum is 1.38.

The previous calculation becomes

$$\frac{1.38}{r_0^2} = \frac{2r_{mol}^8}{r_0^{10}}$$

$$r_0^8 = 1.45\, r_{mol}^8$$

$$r_0 = 1.05\, r_{mol}$$

$$= 0.248 \text{ nm}$$

particular Cl^- ion; the binding energy *per ion* is the depth of the potential well applicable to the solid, whereas the latent heat will be a measure of the binding energy of an *ion pair* in the crystal. These differ by the amount of energy required to separate the ion pair, which was calculated in Section 2.3.1 to be 8.2×10^{-19} J.

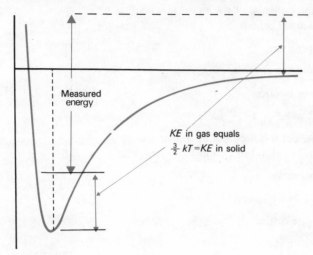

Figure 10 *Measured latent heat is independent of molecular kinetic energy.*

However, we are in a position to get a relationship between the binding energy per ion in the solid and the latent heat of sublimation. From equation (2), we have the potential energy of the free NaCl molecule as

$$V(r)_{r=r_{mol}} = \frac{-e^2}{4\pi\epsilon_0 r_{mol}} \left\{ 1 - \frac{1}{9} \right\} = -0.89 \frac{e^2}{4\pi\epsilon_0 r_{mol}}$$

and for each ion in the lattice, from equation (iii)

$$V(r)_{r=r_0} = \frac{-e^2}{4\pi\epsilon_0 r_{mol}} \left\{ \frac{1.75}{1.17} - \frac{6}{9.1 \times 17^9} \right\} = \frac{-1.33\, e^2}{4\pi\epsilon_0 r_{mol}}$$

(remember, we calculated the equilibrium spacing, r_0, in the crystal to be $1.17 r_{mol}$).

Thus, the energy needed to sublime a crystal containing N ions is

$$(1.33N/2)\, (e^2/4\pi\epsilon_0 r_{mol})$$

the extra factor of 2 in the denominator being there to avoid double-counting the bonds, as explained earlier.

This amount of energy puts the N ions at infinity with respect to each other. They can now be brought together to form $N/2$ molecules with ion separation r_{mol}. In forming these molecules, $0.89\, N/2\, (e^2/4\pi\epsilon_0 r_{mol})$ of energy is released.

Thus, the latent heat becomes:

$$(1.33 - 0.89)\, \frac{N}{2} \left(\frac{e^2}{4\pi\epsilon_0 r_{mol}} \right) = \frac{0.22\, Ne^2}{4\pi\epsilon_0 r_{mol}}$$

Finally, dividing by N, we get the latent heat per ion $-0.22\, e^2/4\pi\epsilon_0 r_{mol}$, which is only about 1/6 of the binding energy of each ion in the crystal.

We might tackle metals in much the same way. If we regard a metal as an assembly of positive ions and negative electrons, then sublimation could be thought of as taking place in two steps. First, the separation of all the ions and electrons to infinity, a process which requires energy; second, the recombination of ions and electrons (one of each for a monovalent metal) to form the atoms which the vapour actually comprises. As with the recombination of Na^+ and Cl^- ions, this process *yields* energy. The measured latent heat, L_s, would then be

L_s = (energy required to remove an ion from the lattice)
   + (energy required to remove an electron from the lattice)
   − (energy given up when an ion and an electron recombine)

It is the first of these three terms which expresses the binding energy of the ions in the lattice, i.e. ϵ. So, to find ϵ, we need L_s and values for the other two terms. These can be found: the energy needed to remove an electron from the metal is measured by finding the minimum photon energy ϕ which will cause electrons to leave the metal (the photo-electric effect); and the energy given up when an ion and an electron recombine is the ionization potential of the atom (I). Then $\epsilon = L_s + I - \phi$. The data is available for the metal cesium

$$L_s = 5.2 \times 10^{-19} \text{ joule per atom}$$

$$I = 6.2 \times 10^{-19} \text{ joule for one electron}$$

$$\phi = 2.9 \times 10^{-19} \text{ joule per electron}$$

$$\therefore \quad \epsilon = (11.4 - 2.9) \times 10^{-19} = 8.5 \times 10^{-19} \text{ joule}$$

In this example ϕ and I are similar, so $L_s \approx \epsilon$, but this need not be so, particularly if the metal atoms are doubly ionized in the solid. For example zinc has

$$L_s = 2.0 \times 10^{-19} \text{ joule per atom}$$

$$I = 43.9 \times 10^{-19} \text{ joule for two electrons}$$

$$\phi = 5.5 \times 10^{-19} \text{ joule per electron}$$

so $\quad \epsilon = 40.4 \times 10^{-19}$ joule which is nowhere near L_s.

Even if the lattice of ions is 'perfect', the electrons in the solid cannot be treated as fixed particles. The Pauli principle demands that they shall have very high kinetic energies (see TS 251*, Unit 4, for example). Consequently, we cannot make a calculation comparable with that for ionic solids, in which both the positive and negative constituents could be regarded as fixed. It is, therefore, a matter of extreme complexity (and quantum rather than classical physics are essential) to get even an approximate theoretical value for ϵ. Thus we cannot compare our experimental value with any simple theoretical prediction.

7.4.2 ϵ from surface energy measurements

Imagine a solid rod being broken. At the break, new surfaces are formed, and to make these surfaces atoms have had to be separated from one another. Energy is therefore expended in creating surfaces. If the spacing of atoms forming the rod is r_0, there are about $1/r_0^2$ atoms per unit area of cross-section. After the rod is broken, each atom in the surface has $\frac{1}{2}\tilde{n}$ nearest neighbours (on average), rather than $\tilde{n}$ in the unbroken solid. So, by breaking $\tilde{n}/2 \times 1/r_0^2$ bonds, two unit areas of new surface are created (one unit area on each part of the broken rod). To break one bond requires energy ϵ, so the surface energy per unit area is

$$\gamma = \frac{\tilde{n}\epsilon}{4r_0^2} \tag{5}$$

This equation provides a direct method of getting ϵ for metals; the atoms at the new surfaces are still ionized, so the problems met in trying to relate ϵ to latent heat measurements are overcome. However, there are new worries—is the surface of the metal anything like the interior in terms of interatomic forces? Measurements of surface energy for metals accurate to about 10 per cent have been achieved, e.g. for gold $\gamma = 1.3$ J m^{-2}. Taking $r_0 = 3 \times 10^{-10}$ m and $\tilde{n} = 12$, we get

$$\epsilon = \frac{1.3 \times 4 \times 9 \times 10^{-20}}{12} = 3.9 \times 10^{-20} \text{ J}$$

which is apparently in the right ball park. It is at least an order of magnitude deeper than the well depths quoted in Table 4 (p. 16) for van der Waals solids.

SAQ 4 The equations for L_s and γ derived in the text refer to spherical atoms. This SAQ asks you to contemplate disc-shaped molecules, for which the derived equations will not do.

Suppose a substance has disc-shaped molecules of radius r and thickness $r/10$. Further suppose that the depth of the potential well for a pair of these molecules depends on their orientation: let it be ϵ for molecules touching face to face and

* The Open University (1973) TS251 *An Introduction to Materials*, The Open University Press.

$\epsilon/30$ for molecules touching edge to edge. Imagine how such molecules might pack together in a crystal and then:

(a)   Estimate the molar latent heat of sublimation.

(b)   Determine which crystal surfaces will be large (i.e. how will the molecules prefer to be packed near a crystal surface).

7.5   The mechanical properties of perfect solids

The internal structures, latent heats and surface energies of solids are not matters of obviously immediate interest to people who *use* solids to *make* things. A blacksmith just knows by experience how thick a piece of iron he needs to make, say, a towing bar, and how hot it has to be for him to be able to hammer one end of it flat. Properties like strength, elasticity and ductility are of much more obvious value. There was a time when the knowledge of blacksmiths, stonemasons and carpenters, each working with one of the three structural materials available, was enough. Now, however, we have a much wider range of materials to choose from and we make much greater performance demands of the materials. No combination of wood, stone and iron will build a 500 MW electricity generator, though these materials made good windmills. It therefore behoves us to try to use our theoretical ideas of the perfect solid in an attempt to gain predictive understanding of the mechanical properties of real solids. The essential point is that we cannot now afford a thousand years and a thousand mistakes in getting enough experience to build large electricity generators (or anything else). Hence *predictive* power, not the hindsight of experience, is needed. The remainder of this Unit is devoted to describing this endeavour.

When a force is applied to a solid, the solid may break or not break. If it does not break, it will deform in response to the force. If the force is removed the solid will either spring back to its original shape (elastic behaviour*) or it will be left in some new shape (plastic behaviour). Which happens depends upon the type of solid and the size of the force. In the following Sections of this Unit, I will treat elastic properties first, then deal with solids which break, and finally examine how plastic deformation can happen. But, before embarking on this project, it is necessary to establish the meanings of some macroscopic parameters which are measurable in laboratories rather than felt by blacksmiths.

7.5.1   The elastic moduli

Deforming forces can be applied to a solid in three distinct ways as shown in Figure 11. There are stretching, shearing, and compressing forces. Stretching requires a linear tension which extends the solid; shearing is the application of tangential forces which would change the angles at the corners of a block; and compression involves forces pressing inwards on the solid from all directions**, trying to decrease the volume of the solid.

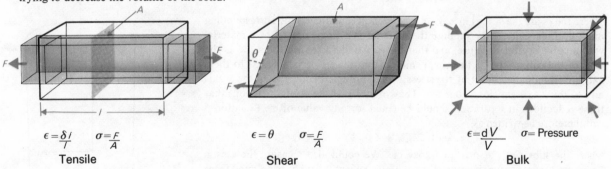

$$\epsilon = \frac{\delta l}{l} \qquad \sigma = \frac{F}{A}$$
Tensile

$$\epsilon = \theta \qquad \sigma = \frac{F}{A}$$
Shear

$$\epsilon = \frac{dV}{V} \qquad \sigma = \text{Pressure}$$
Bulk

Figure 11   The three modes of stress.

* The reversible, 'elastic', behaviour is usually limited to small deformations (bent nails don't unbend when you take the hammer off). The everyday use of the word elastic meaning 'like rubber' contains the idea of reversible deformation but implies recovery from large deformations. This peculiar property of rubber is not typical of solids, and rubber is certainly not classifiable as a 'perfect' solid.

** This is a 'hydrostatic' stress, being identical to the forces experienced by a body wholly immersed in a fluid to such a depth that the dimensions of the body are small compared to the depth of immersion.

The response of a piece of solid to any of these forces depends on the geometry of the piece; for example, a tensile (stretching) force of one newton will have rather less effect on a 10 mm diameter iron bar than on a 0.1 mm diameter iron wire. And further, suppose the wire was stretched by 1 mm by one newton, is this independent of the length of the wire?

QUESTIONS (revision of TV2)

1   Is more force required to stretch a long line of atoms by 1 mm, than to stretch a short line of atoms by the same amount?

2   Is more force required to stretch a long line of atoms by 1 per cent of its original length, than to stretch a short line of atoms by the same fraction of *its* original length?

Answer these questions in terms of forces between atoms.

ANSWERS

1   Let there be N atoms at spacing a mm in the long line. The line's original length is Na mm and its final length $(Na + 1)$ mm. The distance between successive atoms is then $(a + 1/N)$ mm. Let the short line of atoms contain $\frac{1}{2}N$ atoms. Original length $= \frac{1}{2}Na$ mm, final length $= (\frac{1}{2}Na + 1)$ mm. $\therefore$ New distance between successive atoms

$$= \left(\frac{\frac{1}{2}Na + 1}{\frac{1}{2}N}\right) \text{mm} = (a + 2/N)\,\text{mm}$$

The atoms in the short line of atoms have to be pulled further apart than those in the long line. This requires a larger force.

2   The lengths become for the long line; original Na mm; final $1.01\,Na$ mm; new length between atoms $= 1.01\,a$ mm. For the short line, the original length is $\frac{1}{2}Na$, the final length $1.01\,Na/2$ mm and the new bond length

$$\frac{1.01\,Na/2}{N/2} = 1.01a\,\text{mm}$$

which is the same as for the long line. Thus the force required is the same for both lines in this case.

The dimensions of the specimen can thus be removed if we argue in terms of applied force per unit area (stress) and the resultant *fractional* change in dimensions (strain). For *elastic* deformations of all sorts it found that the strains in a solid are proportional to the applied stress. The constants of proportionality are properties of the material under stress and are known as elastic moduli.

If we stretch a rod, in general it gets thinner. In other words, the response of the material to a tensile stress is *two* types of strain: an elongation strain $\delta l/l$; and a radial strain $\delta r/r$. (The ratio of these two strains is called the Poisson ratio, $v = (\delta r/r)/(\delta l/l)$.) Now we can define the response of the material by an equation which reveals the proportionality of stress σ to strain for each strain, i.e.

$$\sigma_z = C_x\epsilon_x + C_y\epsilon_y + C_z\epsilon_z \qquad (6)$$

where the ϵs are the strains in x, y, and z directions and the Cs the corresponding moduli of elasticity. Now suppose the material is a single crystal of a material with a cubic crystal structure, and that the x, y and z axes are the same as the axes of the cube. What is then happening is that planes perpendicular to the z axis are being pulled apart by the stress, while those perpendicular to the x axis and to the y axis get closer together. The symmetry of the crystal demands that these reductions in separation should be equal for any value of σ_z. Equation 6 can therefore be written as

$$\sigma_z = 2C_t\epsilon_t + C_z\epsilon_z$$

where the subscript t stands for transverse. We could also measure the elastic shear modulus, C_s, for the crystal, or more specifically for shearing cube faces relative to one another. We could do this for the faces perpendicular to the z axis by twisting the sample and, again because of symmetry, the result would apply to other directions in the cube. Now the remarkable point is that if interatomic forces are 'central forces'*, it can be shown for cubic crystals that

$$C_t = C_s$$

* (a) Apparently emanating from a point; (b) having the same magnitude/distance relationship in all directions from that point.

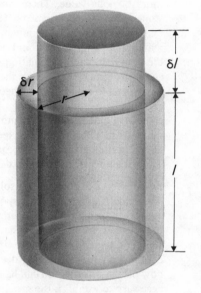

Figure 12   Defining longitudinal and radial strains.

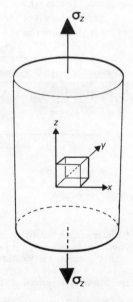

Figure 13   Relating crystal axes to strain axis.

This is an easily tested relationship which can give us information about the nature of interatomic forces in solids held together by various types of force. Table 4 lists this data for some classes of solids which have cubic crystals.

Table 4

Substance	$C_t/10^{11} \text{N m}^{-2}$	$C_s/10^{11} \text{N m}^{-2}$	C_t/C_s
Ionic solids			
LiF	0.54	0.53	1.02
Na Cl	0.127	0.128	0.99
KCl	0.062	0.062	1.00
KI	0.043	0.042	1.03
Covalent solids			
Diamond	1.25	5.76	0.22
Si	0.64	0.79	0.81
Ge	0.48	0.67	0.72
FCC metals			
Cu	1.21	0.75	1.62
Ag	0.90	0.44	2.04
Al	0.62	0.28	2.22
Pb	0.41	0.14	2.83
BCC metals			
Na	0.042	0.049	0.86
K	0.037	0.026	1.42
Fe	1.41	1.16	1.22
W	1.98	1.15	1.72
Van der Waals solids			
Ne	0.0074	0.0060	1.23
Ar	0.015	0.012	1.25

Which groups of solids are bound by central forces?

Only ionic solids.

The success of this test for ionic solids is the justification for our having assumed central forces in the calculation of the Madelung sum in Section 7.3.2.1. The consequence of non-central forces was seen for the van der Waals solids when we tried to predict their crystal structure (Section 7.3.1).

The clear indication that the forces are non-central in metals and covalent crystals presents us with problems. Superficially, the forces binding metal atoms together appear to be isotropic, in that close-packed crystal structures are common among metals. It appears that the naïve criteria in Section 7.2 for close-packed structures are inadequate. Indeed, that many metals pack bcc (which is not a close-packed structure—see SAQ 1, p. 8) shows an immediate defect in the naïve expectation expressed earlier. This is just another manifestation of the problems we met in trying to relate ϵ and L_s for metals.

For the covalent solids, and in particular for diamond, the problem is alleviated by our knowledge of the precise directions of the bonds between atoms. In diamond, the force which is the chemical bond between two neighbouring atoms acts along the line of atomic centres, and we can formulate a pair-potential function (the Morse potential function, Section 7.7.1) which describes the variation of the force along this line. However, the evidence of the elastic constants warns us that we may not assume the same function holds for distant-neighbour interactions *because these are not due to forces acting along the direction of the chemical bond.*

Crystalline solids in general use are not single crystals but are conglomerations of minute crystals more or less randomly oriented. The directional differences in elastic modulus found with single crystals are then averaged out and three moduli, corresponding to the three types of stress, can be specified. It is these 'isotropic' moduli that are usually found tabulated in handbooks. They are

$$\text{Young modulus, } E = \frac{\text{change in tensile force per unit area}}{\text{corresponding fractional change in length}}$$

Shear modulus, $G = \dfrac{\text{change in shearing force per unit area}}{\text{corresponding angular deformation}}$

Bulk modulus, $K = \dfrac{\text{change in pressure}}{\text{corresponding fractional change of volume}}$

For an isotropic solid, E and the Poisson ratio ν define the whole set, since G and K are related to E and ν by

$$G = E/2(1 + \nu) \quad \text{and} \quad K = E/3(1 - 2\nu) \tag{7}$$

Strictly, we should find $\nu = \frac{1}{4}$ exactly for isotropic solids, giving $G = E/3$ and $K = 2E/3$; but in practice ν varies widely (for cork $\nu \approx 0$, for rubber $\nu = 0.5$), though the relations for G and K hold fairly well, given an experimental value for ν.

7.5.2 The interrelation between tensile and shear stresses

A tensile stress applied to a specimen always produces a shear stress inside the specimen. It will be useful to have a quantitative notion of the relative magnitudes of these stresses.

Consider a rod of uniform cross-sectional area A subjected to a tensile force T (Fig. 14a). Inside the rod imagine a thin slice at angle θ to the line of action of T. T may be resolved into components $T \cos \theta$ perpendicular to the slice, and $T \sin \theta$ parallel to the face of the slice. As the diagram shows, the tension T, and hence its components, act in opposite directions on the two faces of the slice. The two components parallel to the faces of the slice are shearing forces acting over the *area of the slice*, so we must find that. Figure 14b shows an edge view of the slice and a plane normal to the axis of the rod. The trigonometry of this diagram shows $r/x = \cos \theta$, so $x = r/\cos \theta$. Now the slice is an ellipse, and the area of an ellipse is given by $\pi a \times b$ (Fig. 14c). In this case, a becomes r the radius of the rod, and b is the length x in Figure 14b. The area of one surface of the slice is then $\pi \times r \times r/\cos \theta$. But πr^2 is A, the cross-sectional area of the rod, so the area of the slice becomes $A/\cos \theta$.

The shear stress τ due to the components of T parallel to the slice is the tangential force applied per unit area, which is

$$\tau = \frac{T \sin \theta}{A/\cos \theta}$$

But T/A is the tensile stress, σ, so

$$\tau = \sigma \sin \theta \cos \theta = \frac{\sigma}{2} \sin 2\theta \tag{8}$$

The slice was just a figment of our imagination for the above calculation, but in a crystal it can become real and be a layer of atoms.

At what angles must a layer of atoms in a rod lie with respect to a tensile stress to suffer the maximum and minimum shear stresses? What are the maximum and minimum shear stresses?

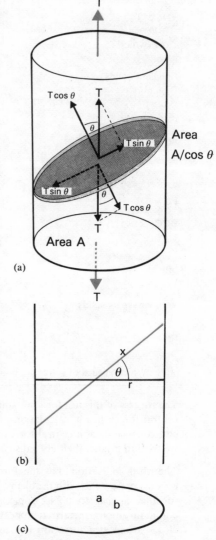

(a)

(b)

(c)

Figure 14   *Resolved shear stress from an applied tensile stress.*

Maximum shear stress (at 45°) is $\tau = \sigma/2$. Minimum shear stress (at 0° and 90°) is $\tau = 0$.

7.6 Bulk moduli of perfect solids

Because all three elastic moduli equations are interrelated by equations 7, it is sufficient to apply theoretical analysis to just one modulus. The bulk modulus, K, is the easiest to consider.

From the definition above, we can write

$$K = -\frac{\mathrm{d}p}{\mathrm{d}V/V} = -V\frac{\mathrm{d}p}{\mathrm{d}V} \tag{9}$$

Where $\mathrm{d}p$ is the change of pressure causing the change $\mathrm{d}V$ in the volume V. The minus sign is merely a convenience to allow K to be a positive number, since an *increase* in pressure causes a *decrease* in volume, $\mathrm{d}p/\mathrm{d}V$ is intrinsically negative.

To relate K to the forces between atoms, we must recognize that the effect of the increased pressure is to push all the atoms slightly closer together than in their unstressed equilibrium spacing. The extra energy dW, contained by the solid is then the work done by the compressing forces:

$$dW = -pdV \tag{10}$$

(dV is negative, but dW is positive, hence the minus sign again.)

dW must be attributed entirely to changes of potential energy of atoms rather than kinetic energy if we are to apply 'perfect' solid theory. Thus, comparison can only be made with experimental results for the adiabatic bulk modulus, i.e. that measured without allowing any heat to flow into or out of the specimen. Experiments at constant temperature are simpler but, provided the temperature is low (which is necessary anyway for the specimen to be approximately 'perfect'), the difference is small.

Equation 10 can be rearranged as:

$$p = -\frac{dW}{dV}$$

and so

$$\frac{dp}{dV} = -\frac{d^2W}{dV^2}$$

then

$$K = V\frac{d^2W}{dV^2} \tag{11}$$

This expression contains only macroscopic terms: V is the volume of the whole specimen and W its total potential energy. Our force equations related to pairs of atoms only, so to relate K to interatomic forces we must recast this last equation into atomic scale parameters. It is convenient to rewrite the derivative d^2W/dV^2 as*

$$\frac{d^2W}{dV^2} = \frac{dW}{dr} \cdot \frac{d^2r}{dV^2} + \left(\frac{dr}{dV}\right)^2 \frac{d^2W}{dr^2} \tag{12}$$

for the following reason. Because we insisted that deformations should be small, the atomic spacing r is close to the static equilibrium value r_0 at which, since this spacing corresponds to the bottom of the interatomic potential energy well, $dW/dr = 0$. The first term on the right of equation 12 may therefore be struck out.

Furthermore, if N atoms are spaced at distance r apart we have

$$V = Nr^3C \tag{13}$$

where C is a numerical factor approximately equal to one, but depending on the type of packing (e.g. $V = Nr^3/\sqrt{2}$ for a close-packed crystal).

$$\therefore \qquad \frac{dV}{dr} = 3Nr^2C$$

$$\therefore \left(\frac{dr}{dV}\right)^2_{r=r_0} = \frac{1}{9Nr_0^4C^2} \tag{14}$$

Substituting equations 12, 13 and 14 into equation 11 gives:

$$K = \frac{Nr_0^3C}{9N^2r_0^4C^2}\left(\frac{d^2W}{dr^2}\right)_{r=r_0}$$

$$= \frac{1}{9Nr_0C}\left(\frac{d^2W}{dr^2}\right)_{r=r_0} \tag{15}$$

It remains merely to express W, the energy of the whole sample, in terms of the two atom interatomic potential.

$$* \frac{d^2W}{dV^2} = \frac{d}{dV}\left(\frac{dW}{dV}\right) = \frac{d}{dV}\left(\frac{dr}{dV} \cdot \frac{dW}{dr}\right)$$

$$= \frac{dW}{dr} \cdot \frac{d^2r}{dV^2} + \frac{dr}{dV} \cdot \left[\frac{d}{dV}\left(\frac{dW}{dr}\right)\right]$$

$$= \frac{dW}{dr} \cdot \frac{d^2r}{dV^2} + \frac{dr}{dV}\left[\frac{dr}{dV} \cdot \frac{d}{dr}\left(\frac{dW}{dr}\right)\right]$$

$$= \frac{dW}{dr} \cdot \frac{d^2r}{dV^2} + \left(\frac{dr}{dV}\right)^2 \cdot \frac{d^2W}{dr^2}$$

Again considering only nearest-neighbour interactions, N atoms each with $\tilde{n}$ neighbours are linked by $\frac{1}{2}N\tilde{n}$ bonds so:

$$W = \frac{1}{2}N\tilde{n}V(r)$$

where $V(r)$ is the interatomic potential function.

$$\therefore \frac{d^2W}{dr^2} = \frac{1}{2}N\tilde{n}\left(\frac{d^2V(r)}{dr^2}\right)$$

and

$$K = \frac{\tilde{n}}{18r_0 C}\left(\frac{d^2V(r)}{dr^2}\right)_{r=r_0} \qquad (16)$$

This expression can now be used with any $V(r)$; let us look at van der Waals solids and at ionic solids.

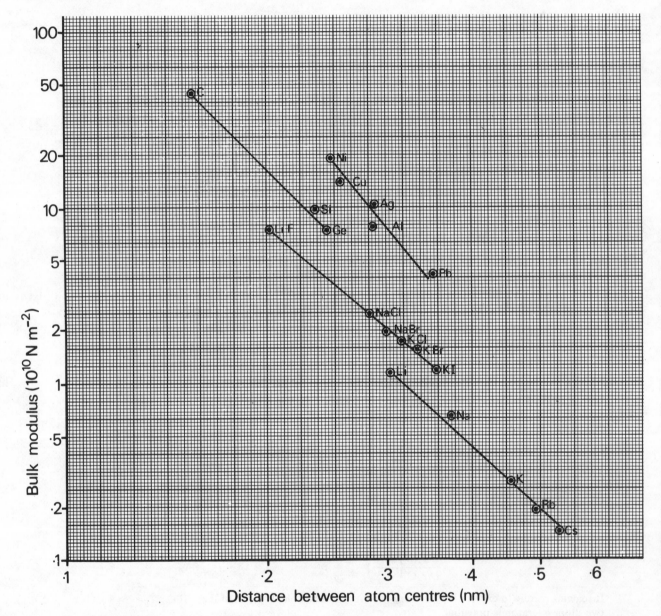

Figure 15 *Bulk moduli related to atomic spacing.*

Even with the very general expression of equation 16, we can make some interesting deductions,

$$\left(\frac{d^2V(r)}{dr^2}\right)_{r=r_0}$$

is a measure of the curvature of the bottom of the potential well. If the curvature is sharp, the modulus will be large. One factor determining the sharpness of the well bottom is the size of the atoms, since small atoms will have small r_0, but the curve must then turn upwards very abruptly. Plotting bulk modulus against interatomic distance for various classes of crystal (Fig. 15) reveals this effect and distinguishes between the different $V(r)$ functions applicable to ionic, covalent and metallic crystals. It is apparent that covalent bonds are to be represented by much more sharply curved wells than are ionic bonds; also, to speak of *the* metallic bond and hope thereby to embrace both nickel and cesium would be over optimistic.

> SAQ 5   Arrange the elements (1–9) listed below into a diagram showing how the bulk modulus (K) of a solid is related to the pair-potential function $V(r)$ appropriate to its atoms.
>
> 1   Relate $V(r)$ to total crystal potential energy W by counting bonds between atoms.
>
> 2   Find the expression $(dr/dV) = f(r)$.
>
> 3   Express d^2W/dV^2 in terms of dW/dr, d^2W/dr^2 and dr/dV.
>
> 4   The definition of K is $K = -V\,dp/dV$.
>
> 5   Set $(dW/dr)_{r=r_0}$ to zero, because at $r = r_0$ crystal potential energy is a minimum.
>
> 6   Extract expression for K in terms of $d^2V(r)/dr^2$.
>
> 7   Derive molar volume V from known crystal structure and interatomic spacing (r).
>
> 8   Equate dW to $-p\,dV$ and hence establish $K = V\,d^2W/dV^2$.
>
> 9   Express d^2W/dr^2 in terms of $d^2V(r)/dr^2$.

7.6.1   Bulk modulus of van der Waals solids

The Lennard-Jones potential appropriate for atoms interacting by van der Waals effects has been shown (Section 7.3.1) to be

$$V(r) = \epsilon\left[\left(\frac{r_0}{r}\right)^{12} - 2\left(\frac{r_0}{r}\right)^{6}\right] \tag{1}$$

To calculate K we want $d^2V(r)/dr^2$ and this is

$$\frac{d^2V(r)}{dr^2} = \epsilon\left[\frac{12.13\,r_0^{12}}{r^{14}} - \frac{2.6.7\,r_0^{6}}{r^{8}}\right]$$

Setting $r = r_0$ yields

$$\left(\frac{d^2V(r)}{dr^2}\right)_{r=r_0} = \frac{72\epsilon}{r_0^2}$$

so

$$K = \frac{\tilde{n}}{18\,r_0 C} \times \frac{72\epsilon}{r_0^2} = \frac{4\tilde{n}\epsilon}{r_0^3 C}$$

But molar latent heat of sublimation L_s is $\frac{1}{2}N_A\tilde{n}\epsilon$ (Section 7.4.1) and the molar volume V_0 is $N_A r_0^3 C$ so we also have:

$$K = \frac{8L_s}{V_0}$$

Alternatively we could write $\tilde{n}\epsilon/r_0^2 = 4\gamma$ (γ = surface energy (Section 7.4.2) and have

$$K = \frac{16\gamma}{r_0 C}$$

Collecting data from here and there for argon, I have found:

$$L_s = 7.6 \times 10^3 \text{ J mol}^{-1}$$

$$V_0 = 22.4 \times 10^{-6} \text{ m}^3 \text{ mol}^{-1}$$

$$r_0 = 0.38 \times 10^{-9} \text{ m}$$

$$\gamma = 38 \times 10^{-3} \text{ J m}^{-2}$$

$$C = 1/\sqrt{2}$$

Whence

$$8L_0/V_0 = 2.7 \times 10^9 \text{ Nm}^{-2}$$

$$16\gamma/r_0 C = 2.25 \times 10^9 \text{ Nm}^{-2}$$

and

$$K = 2.5 \times 10^9 \text{ Nm}^{-2} \text{ by direct measurement.}$$

As γ isn't the easiest thing to measure, it is perhaps justifiable to look proudly at the level of agreement rather than carp over the scatter.

7.6.2 Bulk modulus of an ionic solid

In Section 7.3, we set up a potential function (equation 3) for ions in sodium chloride. The short-range repulsive forces were taken over the six nearest neighbours only on the grounds that the power of r in this term was so high (9) that more distant effects would be entirely negligible compared with the electrostatic interaction. However, this power of 9 was assumed rather arbitrarily, so I will arrange this next calculation as an attempt to find the correct value for this exponent. Let us, therefore, develop the potential function with the repulsive term going as $1/r^p$ where p is the number to be determined.

The potential function can then be written as

$$V(r) = -\frac{1.75\,e^2}{4\pi\epsilon_0 r} + \frac{6A}{r^p} \tag{17}$$

and our first task is to evaluate the constant A. You will remember that we did this for a NaCl molecule in Section 7.3, and the same method applies here; $dV(r)/dr = 0$ at $r = r_0$, the equilibrium spacing of ions in the lattice.

Now
$$\frac{dV(r)}{dr} = +\frac{1.75\,e^2}{4\pi\epsilon_0 r^2} - \frac{6Ap}{r^{p+1}}$$

$\therefore$ at $r = r_0$,
$$\frac{1.75\,e^2}{4\pi\epsilon_0} = \frac{6Ap}{r_0^{p-1}}$$

so
$$6A = \frac{1.75\,e^2}{4\pi\epsilon_0}\frac{r_0^{p-1}}{p}$$

and
$$V(r) = \frac{-1.75\,e^2}{4\pi\epsilon_0}\left\{\frac{1}{r} - \frac{r_0^{p-1}}{pr^p}\right\}$$

which looks tidier if we multiply the contents of the bracket by r_0 (and of course divide by r_0 outside the bracket). Because $r_0 \times r_0^{p-1} = r_0^p$ we then get

$$V(r) = \frac{1.75\,e^2}{4\pi\epsilon_0 r_0}\left\{\frac{r_0}{r} - \frac{1}{p}\left(\frac{r_0}{r}\right)^p\right\} \tag{18}$$

To find the bulk modulus we need $(d^2V(r)/dr^2)$ at $r = r_0$:

$$\left(\frac{d^2V(r)}{dr^2}\right)_{r=r_0} = -\frac{1.75\,e^2}{4\pi\epsilon_0 r_0^2}\left\{\frac{2}{r_0^2} - \frac{(p+1)}{r_0^2}\right\}$$

$$= -\frac{1.75\,e^2}{4\pi\epsilon_0 r_0^3}\left(1 - p\right) \tag{19}$$

We need a value of C (equation 13) for this crystal. A mole of NaCl contains $2N_A$ ions where N_A is Avogadro's number. Thus if the ion spacing is r_0 the molar volume is

$$V_0 = 2N_A r_0^3$$

i.e. $C = 2$, a fact which you can check using Figure 5a.

Equation 15 therefore becomes

$$K = \frac{(d^2W/dr^2)_{r=r_0}}{18Nr_0} \tag{20}$$

There is a subtle distinction between our present calculation and that just done for the van der Waals solid. The Lennard-Jones potential function tells us the potential energy one atom possesses by virtue of its position relative to *one* other atom. We therefore had to count how many neighbours ($\tilde{n}$) each atom had and established

$$W = \tfrac{1}{2}N\tilde{n}V(r)$$

Our potential function for ions in the sodium chloride lattice *has already done this counting*. We have an expression for the potential energy of an ion in the environment of the whole lattice of ions. This was ensured by the Madelung sum (Section 7.3.2.1) for the Coulomb interaction and by writing $6A$ in the repulsion term at the beginning of this Section. But each ion is itself part of the environment of all the other ions in the lattice so, if we multiplied $V(r)$ by $2\,N_A$ to get the total energy W, we would be counting every ion twice. Therefore

$$W = \tfrac{1}{2}2N_A V(r)$$

$$= N_A V(r) \text{ per mole}$$

$$\frac{d^2 W}{dr^2} = N_A \frac{d^2 V(r)}{dr^2} \tag{21}$$

Substituting equations 19 and 21 into equation 20 we get

$$K = \frac{1.75 \,(p-1)\, e^2}{18 \times 4\pi\epsilon_0 r_0^4} \tag{22}$$

Now here is the necessary data

$$e = 1.6 \times 10^{-19} \text{ C}$$

$$1/4\pi\epsilon_0 = 9.0 \times 10^9 \text{ m F}^{-1}$$

$$r_0 = 2.82 \times 10^{-10} \text{ m}$$

$$K = 3.0 \times 10^{10} \text{ N m}^{-2}$$

so you can work out a value for p.

Is p close to the value assumed earlier?

Yes.

Just as the bulk modulus K can be related to $V(r)$, so can the pressure variation of K, and an alternative equation for p can be established. Now look at these results (due to Slater, 1924):

Substance	LiF	NaCl	KI
p from K	5.8	9.1	10.5
p from pressure dependence of K	14.3	9.8	6.8

It has become apparent that the potential function we have used is inadequate as a general representation of even all alkali halides. Much better agreement with experiment was achieved when the repulsion term of the potential function was expressed as an exponential rather than as an inverse power of r. Thus:

$$V(r) = -\frac{Ae^2}{r} + B\,e^{-r/\rho}\,.$$

It was found that the value of ρ was the same to within a few per cent for all the alkali halides rather than ranging widely as did p.

Incidentally, in Section 7.1, I suggested that we should ignore the van der Waals attractive forces in solids containing any more dominant form of bonding. The consequences amount to only $\tfrac{1}{2}$ per cent error in $V(r)_{r=r_0}$ for LiF but range up to 5 per cent for the cesium salts. The cesium ions are large and contain many electrons, so the Coulomb attraction is reduced, whereas the van der Waals attraction is increased. For NaCl the error is about $1\tfrac{1}{2}$ per cent.

SAQ 6 Explain in a few sentences why a perfect solid model can produce reasonable values for the bulk modulus of crystals.

7.7 The fracture strength of a solid

In this Section, we are going to look again at the idea of pulling a solid apart by applying a large tensile force to a rod. We shall consider what tensile stress is necessary to pull one plane of atoms away from an adjacent plane against the attractive interatomic forces. We shall assume that the planes in question lie perpendicular to the axis of the tensile stress so that this stress is as effective as it can be. Furthermore, we shall, for the time being, ignore any possible effects of the internal shear stresses.

There are two methods of tackling this problem: one is to use arguments based on the surface energy requirements of the new surface formed during fracture: the other is to compute the maximum force of attraction which one atom can exert on another. We shall do both, because I think it is interesting to see what a range of apparently unrelated experimental results can be focused onto a single problem.

The Section will end with a sub-section which shows how to reconcile the rather ambitious theoretical predictions with observed strengths of solids.

7.7.1 Theoretical breaking strength from interatomic potential

Over recent years, the search for ever stronger engineering materials has led to investigations of covalently bonded solids such as boron nitride, silicon carbide, and, of course, diamond. Even apart from the virtues of variety, it seems appropriate to determine breaking strength by using a potential function describing covalent interactions. The idea of this calculation comes directly from the general arguments of Unit 2. Let me remind you, via Figure 16, of the relationship between the interatomic potential and the interatomic force curves. For a given potential function we can calculate both the maximum force one atom can exert on another and the increase in atomic spacing which generates this force. Any further extension will be opposed by a reduced force, so the ultimate strength of the solid should be determined by the maximum interatomic force.

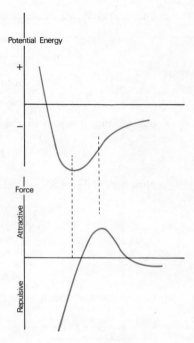

Figure 16 Relationship between potential energy and force curves.

The Morse function is a good representation of a covalent pair interaction. You have not met this function before, it is:

$$V(r) = \epsilon\{e^{-2a(r-r_0)} - 2e^{-a(r-r_0)}\} \tag{23}$$

Unlike Mie's potential function, which uses inverse powers of r, this function uses exponentials. However, its principle is very similar to Mie's; $e^{-2a(r-r_0)}$ varies with r much faster than $2e^{-a(r-r_0)}$, so balancing one term against the other leads to the same familiar shape for a potential function (Fig. 17). The same Figure shows ϵ to be the potential energy of the pair at the equilibrium separation r_0, while a is a constant to be determined.

The force between atoms interacting according to the Morse function is

$$-\frac{d}{dr}V(r) = -\epsilon\{-2a\,e^{-2a(r-r_0)} + 2a\,e^{-a(r-r_0)}\}$$

and this has its maximum value where

$$\frac{d^2V(r)}{dr^2} = 0\,.$$

Now
$$\frac{d^2V(r)}{dr^2} = \epsilon\{4a^2\,e^{-2a(r-r_0)} - 2a^2\,e^{-a(r-r_0)}\}$$

which equals zero if
$$4a^2e^{-2a(r-r_0)} = 2a^2e^{-a(r-r_0)}$$

i.e.
$$2e^{-2a(r-r_0)} = e^{-a(r-r_0)}$$

or by taking logarithms
$$\log_e 2 - 2a(r-r_0) = -a(r-r_0)$$

which reduces to
$$r = r_0 + \frac{1}{a}\log_e 2$$

I will leave you to confirm, by substituting this value of r into $-dV(r)/dr$, that the maximum force is $\epsilon a/2$. Also you should establish that when $r = r_0$, $d^2V(r)/dr^2 = 2a^2\epsilon$. Given these results, we can get a figure for the strength of diamond.

The structure of diamond is shown in Figure 18. Every carbon atom is joined to four neighbours by single covalent bonds. The depth ϵ of the potential well is obtained from thermochemical measurements of the bond strength in any compound containing C–C bonds. In chemical terms, the bond strength is 347 kJ mol^{-1} or $5.8\ 10^{-19}$ joule per bond. The equilibrium length of these bonds is 0.154 nm and this leads to a density of 1.82×10^{19} bonds per square metre between the adjacent planes of Figure 18. It remains to find the constant a.

You know from the TV programme of Unit 6 that the atoms in molecules vibrate, continually stretching and compressing the bonds between them. In that programme, you saw the bonds modelled by springs, and for small amplitude vibrations this is quite an accurate analogy. The force generated in a spring

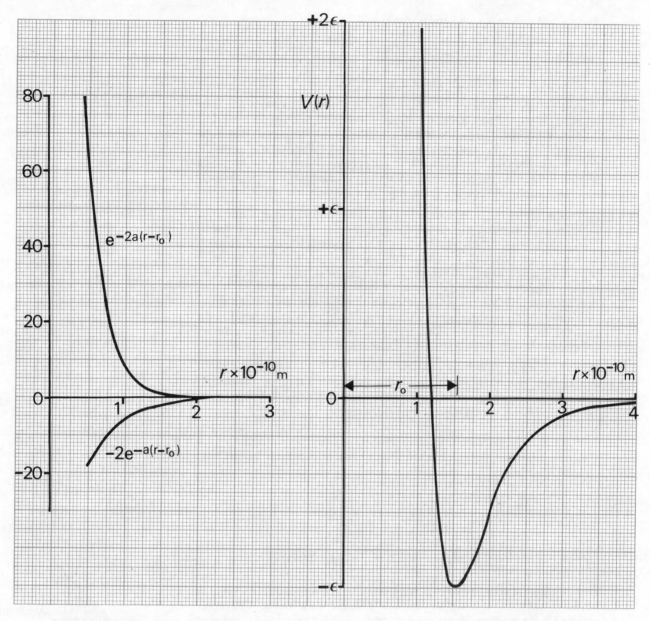

Figure 17 The Morse potential function.

is proportional to its extension (or compression), so when r is approximately equal to r_0 we can write $F = K(r - r_0)$ for the force in the bond; then $dF/dr = K$.

Now, for the interatomic bond, $F = -dV(r)/dr$, so $dF/dr = d^2V(r)/dr^2$. But you have shown that for the Morse function

$$\frac{d^2V(r)}{dr^2} = 2a^2\epsilon$$

So we have $2a^2\epsilon = K$, the constant of proportionality in the spring equation. We can now go a step further. The frequency of the oscillations is determined by the ratio K/m where m is the mass of the vibrating atoms*.

By observing the response of molecules containing the C–C bond to infra-red radiation, this frequency can be found and hence K determined. The value of K is $5.2 \times 10^2\ \mathrm{N\ m^{-1}}$

$$a = \sqrt{\frac{K}{2\epsilon}} = \sqrt{\frac{5.2 \times 10^2}{2 \times 5.8 \times 10^{-19}}}$$

$$= 2.12 \times 10^{10}\ \mathrm{m^{-1}}$$

* Apply Newton's second law to the system (Fig. 19) and $m\ d^2x/dt^2 = -Kx$
then $x = x_0 \sin \omega t$, where $\omega = \sqrt{K/m}$.

The frequency of oscillation is $\omega/2\pi$.

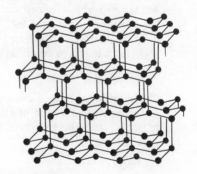

Figure 18 The crystal structure of diamond.

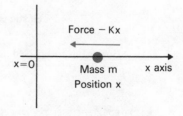

Figure 19

29

The maximum force in each bond is then

$$F_{max} = \frac{\epsilon a}{2} = \frac{5.8 \times 10^{-19} \times 2.12 \times 10^{10}}{2}$$

$$= 6.1 \times 10^{-9} \text{ N}$$

Thus, to break the 1.82×10^{19} bonds per square metre between atoms in adjacent planes and so fracture the crystal, a predicted force of $1.82 \times 6.1 \times 10^{10}$ N is required, that is, the tensile strength of diamond is predicted to be 11×10^{10} N m^{-2}. The observed maximum strength of diamond is 6×10^{10} N m^{-2}, so the theoretical prediction is amazingly precise. It may also be surprising to realize that you can combine X-ray diffraction methods, thermochemistry and spectroscopy and produce a figure for the maximum strength of a solid!

Such close agreement is unusual for a bulk crystal, and diamond is scarcely a common constructional material. Usually, it is only 'whiskers' (those special filamentous crystals which you saw in the TV programme for Unit 2) which approach their predicted strength. Much research has been done to see if 'whiskers' can be successfully combined with metals or resins to make ultra-strong composite materials. If you have studied T100, you will remember, however, that ultimate strength is not the only consideration for a useful engineering material; toughness, which we may loosely define as the capability of a material to absorb energy without breaking is often more important. For further information, if you are interested, references are given below*.

To go further and discover why ordinary solids (if we regard whiskers as 'extraordinary') do not live up to their theoretical promise, it will be very convenient if we can express the theoretical strength in terms of macroscopic parameters, rather than the atomic scale parameters this subsection has required.

> SAQ 7 Use the Morse function to calculate:
> (a) the bulk modulus of diamond. Compare your result with the data of Figure 15;
> (b) the theoretical fracture *strain* of diamond;
> (c) the strain predicted at the observed fracture stress.

7.7.2 Theoretical breaking strength in terms of Young's modulus and surface energy

A tensile force applied to a solid causes an extension of the solid, so the point of application of the force moves through a distance and work is done. This energy is stored in the solid until it can store no more; then the solid breaks. We need to calculate the work done by the tensile force and then relate this to the energy of the new surfaces formed when the solid breaks. When the crystal is stretched the extension e, produced by a force F, is proportional to that force. The work done by the force is converted into elastic energy within the crystal and is the area under the force-extension line.

Thus, elastic energy $= \frac{1}{2}Fe$

Now, instead of force, I can use stress, σ, which is force/cross-sectional area A of specimen; and instead of extension, I can use strain ϵ, the fractional change in length, e/l, of the specimen. Then $\sigma = E\epsilon$ defines the Young modulus for the material and

$$\text{elastic energy} = \frac{\sigma A \, \epsilon l}{2}$$

But $A \times l$ is the original volume of the piece of material and $\epsilon = \sigma/E$ so

$$\text{elastic energy per unit volume} = \frac{\sigma^2}{2E} \qquad (24)$$

How is this energy held in the crystal?

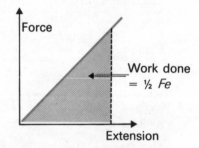

Figure 20 The work done in stretching a sample is the area beneath the force-extension line.

The atoms have been pulled further apart, so the potential energy of each pair of atoms due to their mutual attraction has been increased.

* J. E. Gordon (1968) *The New Science of Strong Materials* Chapter 11. Penguin Books; A. Kelly (1966) *Strong Solids*, Chapter 6, Oxford University Press.

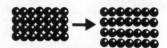

Figure 21

In a perfect solid, a tensile stress must increase the separation between every plane of atoms (Fig. 21), and we have no reason to suppose that the bonds between any given pair of planes will fail before those between any other pair of planes; all planes are identically bonded.

This means that all planes should separate simultaneously and, instead of a long crystal, we would suddenly find that we had a vast number of separated sheets of atoms. We know full well that this is not how crystals break in practice, but it is what the perfect solid model predicts. This is the case we must examine to find a theoretical *maximum* tensile strength for a crystal.

Whatever the nature of the fracture, when it happens, all the elastic strain energy is released, since the force between atoms in adjacent planes falls to zero. Maybe you could think of various ways of dissipating this energy, but provision *must* be made for the energy of the surfaces formed (Section 7.4.2). In the model we have conceived, every plane of atoms would come to have two free surfaces and the energy for these surfaces would have to derive from the elastic energy contained in the volume bounded by adjacent planes of atoms.

If area A of the crystal was broken and a was the atomic spacing in the crystal, this volume would be Aa and the area of new surface formed would be $2A$, so we could set

$$\frac{\sigma_f^2}{2E} \times Aa = 2\gamma A$$

where σ_f is the stress causing fracture and γ is the surface energy

so
$$\sigma_f = \sqrt{\frac{2E\gamma}{a}}$$

This situation would produce the maximum possible surface area on the crystal fragments and so the elastic energy stored before fracture would also be a maximum. The fracture stress deduced from this model is therefore a theoretical maximum value.

Draw a graph of the force separation curve assumed in this analysis. Have we over-estimated or underestimated σ_f?

EXERCISE

Here are some data:

Substance	Young modulus $E/10^{10}$N m^{-2}	Surface energy (γ/J m^{-2})	Atomic spacing (a/nm)
Copper	19.2	1.65	0.21
Zinc	3.5	0.10	0.24
Diamond	121	5.4	0.16
Graphite	1.0	0.07	0.36
NaCl	4.4	0.12	0.28
Al$_2$O$_3$	46	1.0	0.22

(a) Calculate the theoretical fracture stress for each substance and express this as a fraction of the Young modulus.

(b) How does the prediction for diamond from this data compare with our Morse function calculation?

(c) What range of strengths do these materials cover (i.e. how many times stronger than the weakest is the strongest)?

(d) Can you account for the gross difference of strength between diamond and graphite?

Look at the answers, which are on p. 32.

Look at Figure 22. We have over-estimated σ_f, since force is not expected to be proportional to extension up to fracture. Figure 22 indicates (but doesn't prove) that the effect of the gradually falling *gradient* of the force separation curve is to reduce σ_f by a factor of about 2. Hereafter let us take as a reasonable estimate

$$\sigma_f = \sqrt{\frac{E\gamma}{a}} \qquad (25)$$

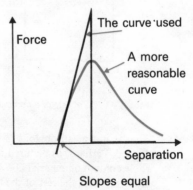

Figure 22 Comparing a simple force-separation curve with a realistic one.

(a)

Substance	Theoretical fracture stress $(=\sqrt{E\gamma/a})$	
Copper	3.9×10^{10} Nm^{-2}	$= E/5$
Zinc	0.38×10^{10} Nm^{-2}	$= E/9$
Diamond	20.5×10^{10} Nm^{-2}	$= E/6$
Graphite	0.14×10^{10} Nm^{-2}	$= E/7$
NaCl	0.43×10^{10} Nm^{-2}	$= E/10$
Al$_2$O$_3$	4.6×10^{10} Nm^{-2}	$= E/10$

(b)   This prediction for diamond is roughly twice that obtained from the Morse function. In view of the rough nature of the model, this factor is not disturbing.

(c)   Diamond is predicted to be 150 times stronger than graphite. The other substances lie between these extremes.

(d)   The great difference of strength between graphite and diamond depends directly on the nature of the interatomic bonds. The graphite structure (Fig. 23) comprises tightly bonded layers of carbon atoms, but the layers are only weakly bonded together. 'Carbon fibres', renowned for their strength, are graphite, but the axis of the fibre is perpendicular to the weak interlayer bands. The fibres are, therefore, strong in tension but can easily bend.

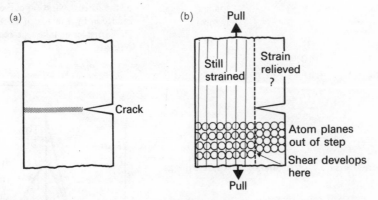

Figure 23   The crystal structure of graphite.

0.142 nm

0.335 nm

The last column of the above table shows the theoretical fracture stress to lie in the range $E/5$ to $E/10$. If we allow another factor of 2, to bring these results into fair accord with calculations from potential functions, the expected strengths are put in the range $E/10$ to $E/20$. However, apart from whiskers, typical fracture strengths are at least an order of magnitude lower than these estimates. Let us go one stage further with the analysis to see why.

7.7.3   Griffith's theory of surface cracks

Some fifty years ago, a scientist named Griffith showed that freshly drawn glass fibres approached the theoretical tensile strength of a perfect solid, but that if the surface was even minutely damaged, by touching the filament say, the strength came plummeting down. Suspecting that surface cracks might be the cause of this effect, he produced a now classic analysis of the effect of cracks.

If the specimen being stretched is cracked (Fig. 24a), it is obvious that the stress in the shaded region is greater than it would be if there was no crack. There are fewer bonds to carry the load.

(a)

Crack

(b)

Pull

Still strained

Strain relieved ?

Atom planes out of step

Shear develops here

Pull

Figure 24   The effects of a notch in a stretched rod.

What is not at all obvious is how the stress through the rest of the crystal is affected. Perhaps, as pictured in Figure 24b, the elastic strain is relieved for the whole column of material above and below the crack and the stress is shared out uniformly over the rest of the cross-section.

If this were so, the planes of atoms in the unstrained and strained parts of the crystal would mismatch at the interface between these regions (Fig. 24b) and shear stresses would arise. Some of the load would then be transferred into the unstrained region.

For cracks of simple shape, the reorientation of stress can be calculated and two significant conclusions emerge.

1   The volume relieved of elastic strain is restricted to a region (of dimensions of the order of the crack depth) around the crack.

2   The stress is *not* uniformly distributed over the uncracked area of the bar, but *is strongly concentrated into the region around the crack tip*. If σ is the stress away from the crack, the stress at the tip of the crack, σ_t, is of the order

$$\sigma_t = \sigma \sqrt{l/r} \qquad (26)$$

where l is the depth of the crack and r the radius of its tip. (This factor $\sqrt{l/r}$ is dependant on the geometry of the crack.)

Visual demonstration of this concentration of stress is provided in Figure 26, where a notched piece of perspex is shown under tensile stress. The refractive index of perspex depends on stress, and arrangements have been made to reveal lines of constant stress. These contours are seen to be bunched around the crack tip.

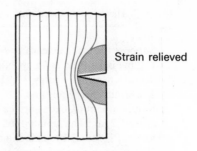

Strain relieved

Consequence of shear

Figure 25   Stress concentration by a notch.

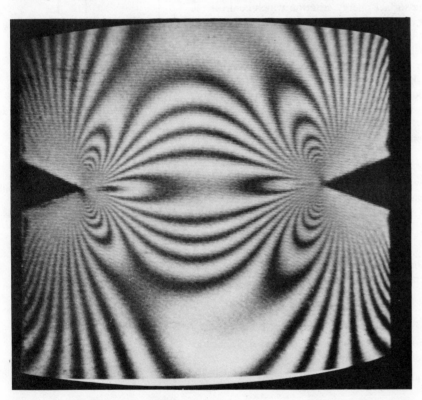

Figure 26   Stress concentrations in perspex revealed under polarized monochromatic light.

Having established the existence of a stress concentration, we can go on under the assumption that our crystal is perfect in all respects other than the presence of the crack. Because of the stress concentration, one set of bonds is carrying more load than all the others so this set will break first, when $\sigma_t = \sigma_f$ i.e., from equations 25 and 26 when $\sigma \sqrt{l/r} = \sqrt{E\gamma/a}$.

Thus a cracked, but otherwise perfect, solid will break (into two pieces, not into separate planes) when subjected to a tensile stress

$$\sigma \geqslant \sqrt{\frac{E\gamma}{l} \times \frac{r}{a}} \qquad (27)$$

You should notice that as the crack propagates l/r increases (l increases, r stays the same), so the stress concentration gets more and more severe. Thus, given a crack for which l/r is big enough to make $\sigma_t = \sigma_f$, the rod should fail. This is an ominous prediction for polycrystalline solids, since the boundary between two crystals could be regarded as a crack so narrow and long that l/r is very large indeed, suggesting a very low strength for such materials. This is not found, so maybe we have left something out of the analysis.

Have you any idea what the extra factor could be?

Suppose the crack extends sideways for unit length (Fig. 27) and that the relieved volume is half that of a cylinder of radius l. This volume is then $1 \times \frac{1}{2}\pi l^2$ and contained strain energy $\sigma^2/2E$ per unit volume before the crack developed. The strain energy released is therefore $\pi l^2 \sigma^2/4E$. If the crack is to grow in length by an amount dl, extra surface of area 1×2 dl will be formed, which will need energy 2γdl. The amount of strain energy released by this growth will be $\pi\sigma^2 ld l/2E$ found by differentiating the strain energy expression just deduced. *The crack can only grow if this released strain energy is enough to provide the surface energy of the new surfaces.* That is, the crack can only grow if

$$\frac{\pi\sigma^2 ld l}{2E} \geqslant 2\gamma d l$$

i.e.

$$\sigma \geqslant \sqrt{\frac{E\gamma}{l} \times \frac{4}{\pi}} \qquad (28)$$

Both the criteria expressed by equations 27 and 28 must be met before the solid breaks. So the criterion determining the fracture stress is the one which requires the higher stress, the other having been satisfied at some lower stress. Whether it is the stress concentration or the surface energy criterion which controls the fracture depends on the value of r/a. According to our equations, if $r/a > 4/\pi$, the stress concentration criterion will be the more difficult to satisfy; if $r/a < 4/\pi$, then the surface energy requirement demands the higher stress. Actually the factor $4/\pi$ comes from some rather vague assumptions about the stress relieved volume and a more realistic threshold for the changeover is $r/a \approx 3$. So, for cracks with tip radius less than about three lattice constants, the surface energy criterion controls the fracture.

What crack property will determine the actual fracture stress if $r \simeq 3a$ (i.e. if both criteria can be met by the same stress)?

As soon as the crack starts to grow, l increases, so more energy is released than is needed for making new surfaces. This surplus energy is dissipated as elastic waves in the crystal. Extra cracks, sound and heat are generated and the solid shatters.

But many solids do not behave like this. It may be true for a ceramic, but it certainly is not so for a metal. The time has now come to build in the shear stress, which accompanies every tensile stress and which we deliberately ignored at the start of this Section.

SAQ 8   Arrange the elements (1–12) listed below into a diagram showing how the theoretical fracture stress (σ_f) of a perfect solid may be expressed. Symbols as in the text (remember, ϵ = strain in this calculation).

1   $2\gamma A$ of surface energy is required for every Aa of solid volume.

2   Young modulus $E = \sigma/\epsilon$.

3   The area under the force-extension curve = the energy stored in elastically stressed bonds.

4   $\sigma_f = \sqrt{2E\gamma/a}$.

5   $\frac{1}{2}Fe = \frac{1}{2}\sigma\epsilon$ per unit volume.

6   $\sigma_f = \sqrt{E\gamma a}$.

7   For a straight line, force-extension curve right up to fracture, the energy stored in bonds = $\frac{1}{2}Fe$.

8   The force-extension curve is non-linear; the straight line estimate of energy is too large.

9   All planes of atoms in a perfect solid should separate at the same stress.

10   The energy stored = $\sigma^2/2E$.

11   Fracture is possible when the elastic stored energy can provide the surface energy of fracture surfaces.

12   $2\gamma A = \sigma_f^2 Aa/2E$.

So far we have only invoked the stress concentration factor and have not considered the size of the region relieved of stress by the crack. This brings us to Griffith's calculation.

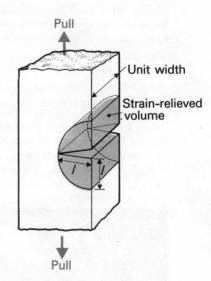

Figure 27   *Griffith's model for the volume of crystal relieved of stress by a notch.*

Its length. If l is large $\sqrt{E\gamma/l}$ is small, so σ_f is smaller for a specimen with deep cracks.

7.8   The shear strength of solids

To achieve a shear deformation (Fig. 11) means that planes of atoms must ride over one another. In this Section, we shall do some rough calculations to see what shear stress is necessary to make a crystal undergo a permanent shear deformation.

To make a start, we shall consider the variation in potential energy required of an atom if it is to move from one lattice site to another. Figure 28 shows a fixed plane of atoms 1, 2, 3 etc. and a representative atom, labelled A, of the next plane up in the crystal. Suppose that the stable crystal structure has A immediately above atom 2 of the fixed layer. A is then in a potential well whose depth is primarily determined by the interaction between A and 2, but which is also influenced by interactions of A with 1 and with 3 and, to a smaller extent, by more distant atoms in the plane. On the diagram are sketched the potential wells which atoms 1, 2, 3 and 4 present to A as it moves above the plane. As drawn, when A is immediately above 2, the interaction with 2 contributes -5 units to A's potential energy; atoms 1 and 3 each contribute -1 unit of potential energy; and atoms 0 and 4 each -0.1 unit. The potential energy of A is -7.2 units. Then, if A moves to A', atoms 2 and 3 each contribute equally to the potential energy at -2.5 units; 1 and 4 each provide -0.4 units so the resultant potential energy is -5.8 units. All these figures are, of course, quite arbitrary and depend only on how I sketched the curves. However, they serve to demonstrate two generalities: that atoms in the upper plane move in a potential, which is periodic in distance x (let us call it $V(x)$); and that the force ($-dV(x)/dx$) on the moving atom is a maximum somewhere between positions A and A'.

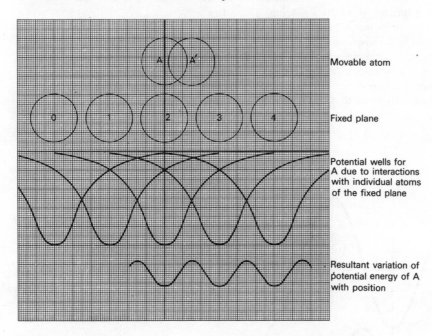

Figure 28   An atom moving above a line of atoms experiences a periodic variation of potential energy which is the sum of the pair-potentials of the moving atom with every atom in the line.

Having decided that the displacement of one atom depends on a periodic potential, we can now extend the argument to a whole plane sliding over another whole plane. The simplest assumption we can make is that each plane slides over the one below it, *the planes themselves remaining rigid*. This is rather like shearing a pack of playing cards. In a perfect solid, we have no reason to suppose that one plane will move more than or less than any other plane; they are all identical and suffer identical stress so they will all be displaced by the same amount. We may therefore conduct the analysis for sliding between two adjacent planes.

Let the planes have area A and be subject to a tangential force F (Fig. 29). The shear stress, τ, is then defined as $\tau = F/A$. If the lattice spacing is a and there are N atoms in the plane, we have $A = Na^2$. Also we know that the shearing force will be opposed by a force $-dV(x)/dx$ from every atom. So we can write

$$\tau = -\frac{1}{Na^2} N \frac{dV(x)}{dx}$$

Figure 29   Defining shear stress.

Although we have not expressed V as an analytic function (to do so would involve detailed consideration of the lattice geometry and the interatomic bonding) let us take $V = -V_0 \cos 2\pi x/a$, as a reasonable approximation. This provides a minimum potential energy for zero displacement and for a displacement of one lattice spacing. Then

$$\tau = -\frac{V_0 a}{2\pi a^2}\left(\sin\frac{2\pi x}{a}\right)$$

which we may write as $\tau_m \sin 2\pi x/a$, τ_m signifying the maximum shear stress required to displace the plane of atoms.

To get a value for τ_m, we can resort to macroscopic measurements. For small shear stresses, solids deform elastically (that is, they recover their shape when the stress is removed) and, in this regime, shear strain is proportional to shear stress. Conventionally $\tau = G\theta$ where G is the elastic shear modulus and θ the angular distortion, i.e. the shear strain. Because, in our present calculation, the strain is distributed uniformly between all the shearing planes, the macroscopic result can be applied to our microscopic element. Then, for small displacements x, the shear strain $\theta = x/a$. Furthermore, $\sin 2\pi x/a = 2\pi x/a$ for small angles, so

$$\tau = \tau_m \sin\frac{2\pi x}{a} \approx \tau_m \frac{2\pi x}{a} \quad \text{and} \quad \tau = G\theta = \frac{Gx}{a}$$

so

$$\tau_m = \frac{G}{2\pi}$$

Let us review what this means. In Figure 30, the fixed plane and moving atom of our earlier argument are reproduced, together with a section of the potential energy versus displacement curve and the shear stress function derived from the potential energy curve. τ_m, the maximum shear stress, is needed to move the upper atom from A to A′, about a quarter of a lattice spacing. Thereafter a smaller shear stress will suffice to move on to A″, the position of maximum potential. Beyond A″, the atom will move to its new equilibrium point A‴ without any stress inducement. In practice, of course, we could not vary the applied stress every time the atoms move by a quarter of a lattice spacing. If stress τ_m was needed to start the deformation, this stress would persist and the moving atom, having reached A′, would flick straight on to A‴. Furthermore τ_m would

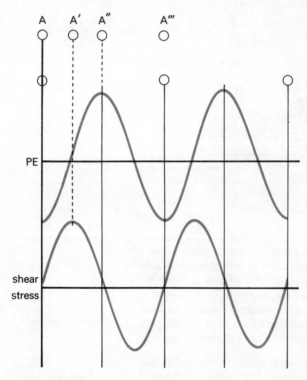

Figure 30 The shear stress necessary to move atom A through successive positions is derived from the periodic potential through which A moves.

still be the applied stress, so the process would repeat again and again. Incidentally, such a shear strain could not be elastic, since the crystal would have achieved a new minimum potential energy configuration (Fig. 31). Thus it would not recover its original shape when the shear stress was removed.

Well, we now have a figure to test against experiment. Is a stress of about $G/2\pi$ needed to produce non-elastic shear in a solid? Typical values of G are around 10^{10} to 10^{11} N m^{-2} so the predicted necessary shear stress is around 10^9 N m^{-2}.

Unfortunately for our model, the limit of elastic deformation comes at shear stresses of 10^5 to 10^6 N m^{-2} a factor of 1 000 below our prediction!

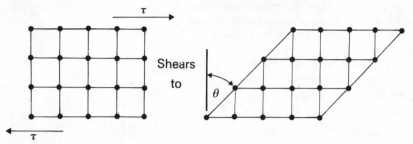

Figure 31   *After a certain amount of shear deformation, a stable crystal structure is re-established.*

However, this model is not entirely fatuous. By searching for lower energy slip paths, in which atoms may zig-zag around their neighbours, and by allowing for some elastic distortion of the planes, it is possible to get τ_m down to about $G/30$. Experiments on whiskers (such as you saw in the TV programme for Unit 2) have given maximum shear stress values approaching 10^{10} N m^{-2}, so in these very special solids our first model is supported.

7.8.1   Crystal twinning

Somehow the mismatch by a factor of 1 000 between prediction and experiment should be expunged. It is clear that the rigid-planes-all-moving-homogenously model is inappropriate for most solids and that we must seek an easier mechanism whereby planes can move over one another. Just before we leave the rigid planes model, however, there remains one possibility of lowering the shear stress needed for permanent deformation; the effect known as 'twinning'.

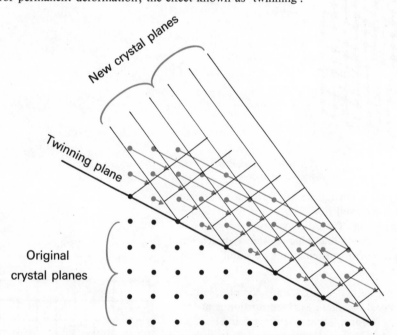

Figure 32   *A possible twinning mode in a two-dimensional crystal. Notice that the new crystal mirrors the old one about the twinning plane.*

In our deduction of the maximum shear stress, we mentioned, but attached no significance to, the movement of all the planes in the crystal. Because a crystal is a geometrically regular array of atoms, it may well happen that by deforming the stable structure we reproduce the same structure in a different orientation. This could happen as a result of quite small displacements of one plane relative to the next, and such displacements may require stresses much lower than that needed to induce a shift of one whole lattice spacing per plane. Fig. 32 shows displacements, capable of producing a twin, in a two-dimensional simple square lattice. You should notice that the twin crystals are mirror images of one another in the twinning plane (marked on the diagram). Since mirror symmetry is the *result* of the twinning process, a necessary condition for twinning is that a twinning plane shall not initially display mirror symmetry. This condition is more easily fulfilled in crystals of low symmetry (e.g. hcp) than in highly symmetric crystals (e.g. fcc). Do you remember the demonstration of 'twinning noise' on the introductory tape? The metal used was cadmium and this has hcp structure.

A symmetry condition alone is not sufficient to determine whether a crystal *will* deform by twinning, but it does imply that if twinning has occurred once on a given set of planes, it cannot happen again—because the twin configuration possesses mirror symmetry. The amount of shear strain produceable by twinning is therefore limited. It should be possible to evaluate a critical shear stress for a perfect solid twinning in a particular geometry. Experiments show that we need not bother to try! Twins form only because of imperfections in the crystal structure, so we can conclude that the critical shear stress for twinning in a perfect crystal is also higher than that observed in real solids.

7.8.2 Shear deformation by dislocation movement

The reason that our original model predicts such a high shear stress for permanent deformation is that each atom in a plane is required to climb out of its potential well at the same time as all the others. If a mechanism existed where only a few atoms at a time were displaced, the stress requirement should be reduced. Such a mechanism is indeed possible because the planes of atoms are capable of elastic deformation. Forces applied as in Figure 33 could compress part of the crystal while leaving the rest in perfect register. However, there is still a large proportion of the crystal deformed at any one time. In fact, the region of com-

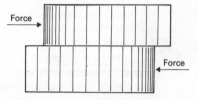

Figure 33 *Exaggerated model showing shear in an easily elastically deformable block.*

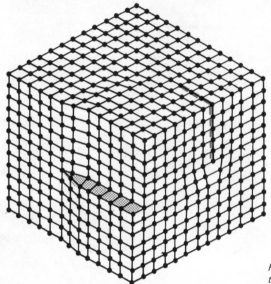

Figure 34 *A dislocated crystal—three-dimensional.*

pression is very restricted and as a crystal is sheared we can arrive at an atomic arrangement like Figure 34. Part of the crystal has slipped one whole lattice spacing and regained crystallographic register. The other part of the crystal has not slipped at all and is therefore also in crystallographic register. Between the slipped and unslipped regions is a band of disorganized atoms, constituting what is known as a 'dislocation'.

The geometry of such distorted regions of the crystal is generally complex, but on the right-hand vertical plane of the crystal in Figure 34 the distortion is not so complicated. For the purposes of this Course, we can restrict our attention to this dislocation geometry; a much more thorough treatment of the geometry and dynamics of dislocations is available in Course TS 251, Unit 6. The simple geometry we are going to use is called an 'edge' dislocation and Figure 35 (which is like the right-hand plane of the crystal in Figure 34) shows that this type of dislocation involves an extra half plane of atoms slipped in between complete planes—like a book-marker in a book.

First let us see how the dislocation can move. The atom marked C is in an unusual situation; it does not have a nearest neighbour at the correct distance immediately above it. Atoms A and B are both at the same distance from C, but at greater than the correct lattice distance, so they are only weakly bonded to atom C. But what will happen if the crystal is sheared as indicated by the arrows? Atom A is being pushed towards C while B is pushed away from C. Atoms A and B need to move only a very small distance for atom C to become definitely bonded to A. D then replaces C as the atom at the centre of the dislocation. The distortion to the left relaxes and that to the right increases. This process can be repeated with D moving its bond to E, making F the atom at the head of the dislocation.

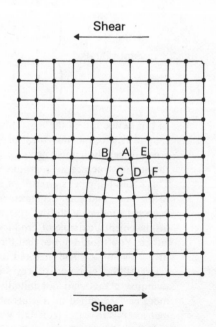

Figure 35 *The simplest dislocation geometry: an 'edge' dislocation.*

So, step by step, the crystal is sheared by one atomic spacing, while the dislocation runs right through the crystal ending up as Figure 36 shows. You might have already realized that, for any substantial shear strain to be produced, there must be a constant supply of new dislocations. There are indeed such sources in real crystals. The argument used to explain the case with which real solids can be sheared relies on the (now well-proven) assumption that dislocations are present in all real crystals even before any attempt is made to shear them and that they are bred by the very act of shearing.

It is not immediately obvious that a dislocated plane can shear more easily than a perfect plane. You will see a model which shows that this is so in the TV part of this Unit, but a simple attempt to calculate the force necessary to displace a dislocation is revealing.

As long ago as 1938, Frenkel and Kontorova proposed a mechanical analogue of an edge dislocation in a one-dimension crystal—i.e. a line of atoms. The atoms are represented by massive points and the bonds within the line become springs in the model. The attraction of atoms in an adjacent line is represented by a 'substrate potential' for which any function can be chosen. This potential could be made to act on the 'atoms' in the line by providing a series of hills and attaching weights to the points representing the atoms. (The model you will see on the TV programme uses a magnetic interaction.) Figure 37 shows the analogue for a 'perfect solid', the springs between atoms are neither stretched nor compressed and the substrate potential of every atom is a minimum—each weight is at the bottom of a hill.

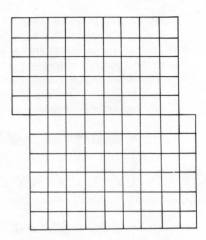

Figure 36 The crystal of Figure 35 after the dislocation has moved right through it. A plastic shear strain has been effected.

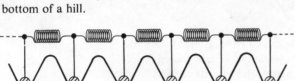

Figure 37 The Frenkel-Kontorova model showing a perfect crystal.

What would happen to such a model if a force was applied to one end of the spring-loaded chain. (Answer in words not as a calculation.)

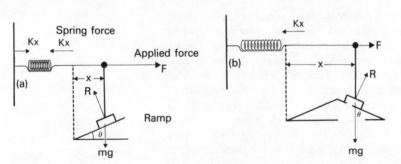

Figure 38 Forces within a single cell the Frenkel-Kontorova model.

Consider the equilibrium in one cell of the model and show that the force transmitted to the next cell is smaller if the weight is still climbing. Use Figure 38 and let the tension in the spring be Kx.

So we see that if the planes are elastic rather than rigid, even a perfect solid could shear easily. This does not help much though, because the bonds between atoms are equivalent to very stiff springs—in other words, the first weight cannot be dragged to the top of its hill without getting all the others well on the way up their hills.

But now look at Figure 39. Here the Frenkel-Kontorova analogue is modelling a dislocation, there being one more 'atom' in the spring-loaded line than there are wells in the substrate potential. There is obviously an energy price to be paid for introducing this extra atom because some of the weights are no longer at the bottoms of the hills and some of the springs are compressed. This need not worry us though, because a real crystal contains dislocations as imperfections of its growth. Our interest lies in whether this system will shear more easily than the perfect system. Figures 39 a, b, and c show the dislocation in successive

The springs would all extend and the weights would all rise, but by progressively smaller increments as you go down the chain. If the applied force is large enough to pull the first weight to the top of its potential hill, this weight will start to go down hill, and will augment the applied force. The increased force will then be able to pull the second weight to the top of its hill, so the applied force will be further increased. Thus, if one weight can get to the top of the hill, the whole line will move one 'atomic spacing'.

The force acting on the next cell is the tension Kx in the spring. Resolving forces on the 'atom' horizontally.

$F = Kx + R \sin \theta$

But $mg = R \cos \theta$

$\therefore Kx = F - mg \tan \theta$

Figure 38a shows that the reaction of the hillside on the weight acts *with* R rather than against F once the top of the hill has been passed. Notice how nasty things would get if K and θ were functions of x. (A potential energy analysis is less messy.)

symmetrical positions, (c) being the same as (a), with the dislocation displaced one atomic spacing down the line. Because of the symmetry, there can be no internal stresses in the model in any of these configurations so, to move from one to the next must require an external stress to be applied. But it is, I think, almost self-evident that *this applied stress can be very small because any weights which have to rise are assisted by those which have to fall and any springs which have to be compressed are helped by the decompression of other springs.*

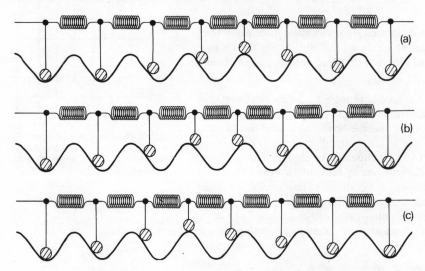

(a)

(b)

(c)

Figure 39   The Frenkel-Kontorova model of a dislocation.

So there is a quantitative agreement. But cannot the model be more use than that? Once a particular substrate potential and spring constant have been chosen, the actual stress requirements can be worked out. But here is where the theoretical problem comes right back to perfect solids theory. You see that the ease of movement of the dislocation depends critically on the height of the substrate potential hills and this has to be calculated from pair-potential functions using more than a nearest neighbour approximation (see Fig. 28). The interatomic force curves are just not defined precisely enough to permit this calculation to be done with enough accuracy.

However, a good theoretician is never put off by such mundane considerations! He will choose 'reasonable' functions and work with those. Any results would then be suggestive of the likely trend of affairs but not directly testable by experiment. Such calculations indicate that the critical shear stress for an edge dislocation is no larger than $G/100$ and rapidly falls to $G/1\,000$ as the width of the dislocation rises. By the 'width' of a dislocation, I mean how many atoms are displaced from perfect register by at least some amount (say 10 per cent of a lattice spacing). It thus becomes clear that the dislocation model can explain the ductility of crystalline materials. We can even argue a bit further now; because the stress needed to shear a dislocated plane depends on the width of the dislocation, we can get a qualitative idea of why some crystals are hard (diamond, sapphire) and some are soft (pure metals). In covalently bonded crystals, which diamond is, the bonds are precisely directed and the energy required to distort them is very large. Dislocations are therefore narrow and consequently difficult to move, therefore diamond is very hard. By comparison, the forces between metal atoms are much less specifically directed, which favours wide dislocations. Metal crystals tend, therefore, to be rather softer.

Another effect which works in the same direction is that wide dislocations can form with lower energy cost on widely spaced planes in the crystal. Now, the closer the packing within a plane, the further away atoms in adjacent planes must lie; so close-packed structures should contain wide dislocations. This again leads to metal crystals being soft.

Yet you will no doubt be thinking that typical metals, as used by engineers, are not particularly soft. Of course, you are right, but it turns out that most of the properties of metals valued by engineers depend upon dislocations. Not upon the presence or the lack of dislocations, but upon whether they can move or not. Most pure metals are soft and ductile but, if the motion of dislocations can be impeded, the metal becomes tough. This is obviously a useful property: the ability to stamp a car body out of a flat sheet of steel depends upon it, and so does the ability of that same car body to survive being knocked about in service, or in the extreme case, absorb all the energy of a high-speed crash. Going a stage further, if the dislocations can be entirely prevented from moving, the metal can be very hard indeed. To effect these property changes involves disrupting the crystalline perfection of the metal quite considerably, so that moving dislocations come against potential barriers which they cannot surmount. This can be done merely by straining a metal (bend a piece of copper pipe of about $\frac{1}{4}$ in diameter and then try to straighten it again). Another method is to alloy two metals together. This is particularly effective if a fine-grained precipitate can be persuaded to form in the metal. Aluminium alloyed with 2 per cent copper contains a dispersion of fine particles of the compound $CuAl_2$. The result is 'duralumin', a much harder and tougher material than pure aluminium. And steels which are alloys of iron and carbon can be modified from being highly ductile, through great toughness, to extreme hardness by changing the quantities and mode of dispersion of the carbon.

But there is another side to this coin. If a metal part has a crack or notch in it, either by damage or design, ductility can save it from breaking by crack propagation. Dislocations can move into the crack, under the influence of the concentrated stress at the crack tip, and blunt the crack. As the crack becomes blunter the stress concentration falls (equation 27), so the dislocations no longer move and the crack becomes stable. Also the Griffith criterion will be changed, since now the released strain has to provide energy for new surfaces *and* for plastic deformation of the crystal at the crack tip. Then, the criteria for crack failure cannot be met and the solid yields plastically (Fig. 40). (But see SAQ 9 for the consequence of dislocations moving *away* from the crack under the stress concentration.) If dislocation movement is difficult, the elastic modulus appears to be high, because slip is inhibited and the crack propagation criteria are easily met, so brittle fracture occurs (Fig. 40). It is really the possibility of cracks becoming stable which distinguishes metals as 'tough' materials.

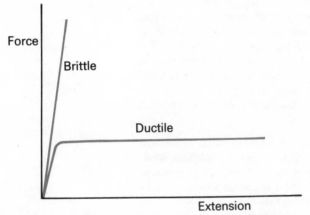

Figure 40   Stress-strain relations for brittle and ductile materials.

SAQ 9   A single crystal of square section (area 1 cm^2) is subjected to a tensile load of 100 kg which is removed and reapplied repeatedly. The crystal has a face-centred cubic structure and the sample shows perfect cube faces except for one face which contains a tiny crack (Fig. 41). The radius of the tip of such a crack may be taken as equal to the lattice spacing a.

When the load is applied, the resolved shear stress on the planes of atoms at 45° angle to the tensile stress causes dislocations to move on these planes. Every pair of dislocations (one from each side) arriving at the crack makes it one lattice spacing deeper, but does not change the crack tip radius. Thus, if n dislocation pairs have arrived, the depth l of the crack will be $l = na$. Furthermore, the number of dislocations moving per loading cycle will depend on the concentrated stress at the crack tip (σ_t), which in turn depends upon the depth of the crack. For the purposes of this question, suppose the number of dislocation pairs moving per loading cycle is σ_t/σ_0, where σ_0 is the applied tensile stress.

You may use the following numerical data:

$a = 2 \times 10^{-10}$ m; $E = 2 \times 10^{11}$ N m^{-2}; $\sigma = \pi/2$ J m^{-2};

and the acceleration due to gravity $= 10$ m s^{-2}

1   How many lattice spacings deep can the crack become before being unstable under the applied load?

2   After how many loading cycles will the specimen break?

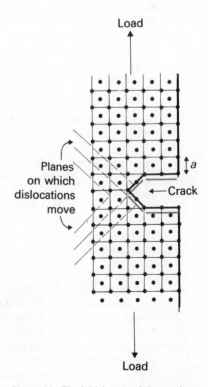

Figure 41   The initial state of the crack (for SAQ 9).

SAQ 10 A close packed-plane of equal-sized atoms lies at an angle of 60° to a tensile stress σ. Using the balls from your Home Kit, or by drawing part of a close-packed plane, you can establish that there are three sets of channels down which atoms could slide. Only the component of the shear stress acting parallel to a channel direction can produce sliding.

Calculate the *minimum* effective shear stress in the plane.

SAQ 11 Sketch curves to show the variation of potential energy with position of an atom moving over a line of atoms when the position of *minimum* potential energy is as A in Figure 28. (You will have to use part of the repulsive force curve in this case.) Is the potential seen by the moving atom similar to the example worked through in the text?

SAQ 12 Explain in about 100 words why pair-potential functions are not very useful in calculations of the stress needed to move a dislocation.

7.9   Conclusion

So let us review our progress in just a few final sentences. At the beginning of this Unit, we defined a perfect solid as one in which we know the positions of the atoms. For practical purposes this meant crystals, and for theoretical purposes it meant we can use pair-potential functions to describe the interactions within crystals, though it soon became clear that many pairs of atoms have to be counted to get a reasonable value for the potential. A brief indication of the problems of the reverse process—deducing potential functions from experimental results—followed.

Solids in use come under various sorts of stress (electrical, magnetic, mechanical, thermal) and it is the responses of crystals to such external stimuli which are of interest. By concentrating on one type of stimulus, we have been able to find out how to use the perfect solid model in ways more subtle than obvious. In particular, having eventually concluded that the mechanical properties of solids depend upon slight *imperfections* of structure rather than perfection, we were able to use results from the perfect-solids approximation to suggest the dynamical properties of these imperfections.

It is, I think, interesting to compare the status of the perfect solids model with that of the perfect gas model. Because the calculations for situations where several atoms interact are less tractable than those for two-atom interactions, the best results derived in this Unit err by several if not some tens of per cent. This is a contrast with the perfect gas theory, which matches real gases so closely that quite minute deviations from ideal behaviour can be used to improve (if necessary) the theory.

One may indeed wonder why the perfect gas theory needs improving. For example, do Gas Board Engineers need to apply more refined theory in order to calculate flow rates of gases through pipelines? I doubt it. True, the perfect gas should never liquefy, which might lead to a serious oversight! But by and large, the tiny interaction between atoms in a real gas produces only minor deviations of properties from those predicted by the perfect-gas theory. By contrast, an engineer believes the theory of perfect solids at his (and our) peril. Tiny amounts of disorder in a perfect crystal can produce enormous effects. To ignore this fact may give us a simple theory, but it is often unuseable. The gross overpredictions of strength would form an insecure basis for structural design.

Not surprisingly, then, many engineers look rather derisively at physicists' models of solids; they know the simple models are wrong and find the complex models either incomprehensible or still of inadequate accuracy. Perhaps it is understandable that engineering is conducted in terms of measured values rather than theoretically predicted ones. But to deride these simple models is to show a lack of appreciation of the inherent difficulties in understanding the solid state and a lack of gratitude for the products (alloys with improved mechanical properties for example) which have been inspired often by deep understanding of atomic-scale processes in solids.

SAQ Answers and comments

SAQ 1

Items 2 and 5 together define a 'perfect solid'. A crystal at low temperature approximates to a perfect solid, since its atoms are almost regularly arrayed and their kinetic energy is much less than their potential energy. Glasses have irregular arrangements of atoms so item 4 is definitely wrong. When melting occurs, kinetic energy approximately equals potential energy so item 6 is also definitely wrong.

SAQ 2

(a) No.

(b) Yes, the body diagonals, of which there are four.

(c) Two; remember that those at the corners are each shared with eight other structure cells so the sum is

$$(8 \times \tfrac{1}{8}) + 1 = 2$$

(d) The body diagonals are two atomic diameters ($2D$) long, so by Pythagoras's theorem (letting the cube edge length = a)

$$a^2 + a^2 + a^2 = (2D)^2$$
$$\therefore a = 2D/\sqrt{3} = 1.155D$$

so the adjacent atoms along the cube edges *do not touch*.

(e) The volume of each atom is $\tfrac{4}{3}\pi(D/2)^2$, so the volume of the two whole atoms per cell is $\pi D^3/3$.

The volume of the cell is $a^3 = 8D^3/3\sqrt{3}$ from section (d) above.

$$\therefore \text{ the fraction of space occupied} = \frac{\pi D^3/3}{8D^3/3\sqrt{3}}$$
$$= \frac{\sqrt{3\pi}}{8} = 0.68$$

(f) Eight.

(g) Six; at distance a, being those in the centres of adjoining cells.

(h) $V_{\text{bcc}} = \epsilon\left\{\dfrac{8}{1^{12}} - \dfrac{2 \times 8}{1^6} + \dfrac{6 \times (\sqrt{3})^{12}}{2^{12}} \right.$
$$\left. - \dfrac{2 \times 6 \times (\sqrt{3})^6}{2^6} \cdots\right\}$$
$$= -11.99\,\epsilon$$

(i) $V_{\text{fcc}} = -15.57\,\epsilon$, i.e. 30 per cent deeper.

(j) No, the fcc well is much deeper than the bcc well (cf. the hcp well, which was effectively equal to the fcc well). This energy difference is large enough to prevent van der Waals bound bcc crystals from forming. In other words, the attractive forces keep on pulling the atoms together until they are close packed.

SAQ 3

Step 1   Convert force, F, to potential $V(r)$

If
$$F \infty r^{-4}$$
$$V(r) \infty \int r^{-4}\,\mathrm{d}r$$

because a force is the differential of a potential

$$\therefore V(r) = cr^3$$

where c is a constant.

Step 2   Set up a series for the potential of a dipole in the line.

$$V(r) = -\frac{2c}{r^3}\left\{1 - \frac{1}{2^3} + \frac{1}{3^3} - \frac{1}{4^3} + \frac{1}{5^3} - \cdots\right\}$$

Step 3   Sum up the series.

The positive terms are 1; 0.037; 0.008; 0.003; 0.001.

The negative terms are 0.125; 0.016; 0.005; 0.002; 0.001.

Hence the series sum is 0.900, and the Madelung sum of $2 \times 0.9 = 1.8$

A double line of charges such as this is a nearer approximation to a real lattice, so the Madelung sum, not surprisingly, is fairly close to the figure for a real lattice.

SAQ 4 The molecules could pack as close-packed planes of discs stacked one upon the other—rather like the graphite structure of Figure 23.

In this case, the coordination number of a molecule will be 8 made up of 6 nearest neighbours within a plane and 2 in adjacent planes.

(a) Estimation of latent heat

To remove one molecule requires that six bonds of strength $\epsilon/30$ and two of strength ϵ should be broken. Thus to evaporate N molecules will require (remembering the $\tfrac{1}{2}$ to avoid double counting of bonds):

$$L = \frac{N}{2}\left(6\frac{\epsilon}{30} + 2\epsilon\right) = 1.1N\epsilon$$

(b) Surface energy

(i) *Exposed surface comprising disc faces*

Figure 42a shows that the area occupied by $\tfrac{3}{6}$ (i.e. $\tfrac{1}{2}$) of a molecule is $\sqrt{3}r^2$ (area of triangle = $\tfrac{1}{2}$ base × height and sin 60° = $\sqrt{3}/2$). The number of molecules per unit area of this surface is therefore $1/2\sqrt{3}r^2$. To make such a surface, one bond of strength ϵ has to be broken for each molecule,

$$\therefore \gamma = \frac{\epsilon}{2\sqrt{3}r^2} = 0.29\frac{\epsilon}{r^2}$$

(ii) *Exposed surface comprising disc edges*

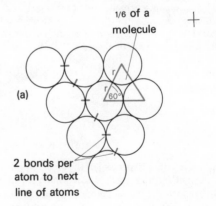

(a)

2 bonds per atom to next line of atoms

(b)

Figure 42

Figure 42b shows the area occupied by one molecule is

$$2r \times \frac{r}{10} = \frac{r^2}{5}$$

$\therefore$ Number of molecules per unit area $= 5/r^2$.

To make this surface, each atom in the surface must be parted from two neighbours (see Fig. 42a) to each of which it has bonds of strength $\epsilon/30$

$$\gamma = 2 \times \frac{\epsilon}{30} \times \frac{5}{r^2} = \frac{\epsilon}{3\,r^2} = 0.33\,\frac{\epsilon}{r^2}$$

Because the surface energy is lower when disc faces are exposed, the crystal should grow with these faces larger.

SAQ 5 The crucial step is number 3, the others supply the relevant expressions for substitution into the result of step 3 to give the result 6. The diagram is:

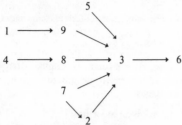

SAQ 6 The small reversible deformations described by the term 'elastic' are achieved by each atom moving a small fraction of an atomic spacing away from equilibrium. The elastic moduli (ratios of stress to strain) are all proportional to the curvature of the bottom of the potential well to these experimental parameters are used to *define* an appropriate potential function—hence the good agreement.

SAQ 7

(a) Equation 16 gives

$$K = \frac{\tilde{n}}{18r_0 C}\left(\frac{d^2\,V(r)}{dr^2}\right) r = r_0$$

From Figure 18, $\tilde{n} = 4$. From Figure 15, $r_0 = 0.154$ nm and from the text $d^2\,V(r)/dr^2 = 5.2 \times 10^2$ N m^{-1} First assume $C = 1$. Then

$$\therefore K = \frac{4 \times 520}{18 \times .154 \times 10^{-9}} = 7.5 \times 10 \text{ N m}^{-2}$$

Observed value = 4.4×10^{11} N m^2.

The discrepancy is mainly due to taking $V = N_A r_0^3$ as the molar volume. Because the directed covalent bonds prevent close packing, the structure is more open than this. Working from the known crystal structure gives

$$V = \frac{8}{3\sqrt{3}} N_A r_0^3 = 1.54\, Nr_0^3$$

Then $$K = \frac{7.5}{1.54} \times 10^{11} \text{ N m}^{-2}$$

$$= 4.9 \times 10^{11} \text{ N m}^{-2}$$

which is within 10 per cent of the observed value! Notice that the potential function method can handle *elastic* properties much better than the fracture properties, and in the case of diamond we were delighted even by the predicted fracture strength.

(b) From text,

the bond length at the theoretical fracture stress = $r_0 + \dfrac{\log_e 2}{a}$

$$\text{Strain} = \frac{\text{Increase in length}}{\text{Original length}}$$

$$= \frac{\log_e 2}{ar_0}$$

$$= \frac{0.69}{2.12 \times 1.54} = 0.21, \text{ i.e. 21 per cent.}$$

(c) The actual fracture stress $\simeq \frac{1}{2}$ theoretical fracture stress so

each bond has developed only half the maximum force i.e. $\epsilon a/4$. But the magnitude of the force in the bond is given by

$$\frac{d}{dr} V(r) = 2\epsilon a\,\{-e^{-2a(r-r_0)} + e^{-a(r-r_0)}\}$$

Thus at the actual fracture stress

$$\tfrac{1}{4} = 2\,\{-e^{-2a(r-r_0)} + e^{-a(r-r_0)}\}$$

Using the recommended approximation we have

$$\tfrac{1}{8} = -1 + 2a(r - r_0) + 1 - a(r - r_0)$$

$$r - r_0 = \frac{1}{8a}$$

$$\text{Strain} = \frac{r - r_0}{r_0} = \frac{1}{8ar_0} = \frac{1}{8.2.12 \times 1.54} = .037$$

$$= 3.7 \text{ per cent}$$

The great difference between the strains calculated in (b) and (c) indicate of how steep sided the potential well is near the region of maximum attractive force. Also, our delight may not extend to the prediction of fracture strain.

SAQ 8 A suitable sequence would be

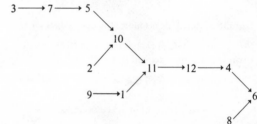

SAQ 9

1   The crack tip radius = lattice spacing (given), so this constitutes a very sharp crack which will propagate when the Griffith criterion is met ($r < 3a$) The stress for failure is

$$\sigma = \sqrt{\frac{E\gamma}{l} \times \frac{4}{\pi}} \qquad \text{(from equation 28)}$$

or, since the applied stress has always the same maximum level (σ_0) the crack length for failure is

$$l = \frac{4E\gamma}{\pi\sigma_0^2}$$

But $l = na$ and n is what we wish to find

$$\therefore n = \frac{4E\gamma}{\pi a \sigma_0^2}$$

Now 100 kg weight = 100 g newtons = 10^3 N.

This force is applied to 1 cm^2 i.e. 10^{-4} m^2 so $\sigma_0 = 10^7$ N m^{-2}. Substituting the other data

$$n = \frac{4 \times 2 \times 10^{11} \times \pi/2}{\pi \times 2 \times 10^{-10} \times 10^{14}} = 20 \times 10^6$$

Incidentally the crack depth is then $20 \times 10^6 \times 2 \times 10^{-10}$ = 4×10^{-3} m, i.e. 40 per cent of the thickness of the bar, so the approximations used in the stress concentration formula (which assumes the crack is in an infinite block) are becoming poor.

2   The stress at the crack tip is

$$\sigma_t = \sigma_0 \sqrt{\frac{l}{r}}$$

$$\therefore \sigma_t = \sigma_0 \sqrt{\frac{na}{a}} = \sigma_0 \sqrt{n}$$

∴ The number of dislocation pairs arriving per loading cycle is

$$dn = \frac{\sigma_t}{\sigma_0} = \sqrt{n}$$

Strictly, the number of cycles of load which will cause failure should now be found, calculating the change of n for every load cycle and counting the number of cycles needed to bring n to 20×10^6. However an integration will suffice. Our equation $dn = \sqrt{n}$ for the change in n per loading cycle can be written $dn/dN = \sqrt{n}$ where dN is the change in the number of loading cycles (i.e. 1). Then

$$\int_0^N dN = \int_0^{20 \times 10^6} \frac{dn}{\sqrt{dn}}$$

$$N = 2\sqrt{20.10^6}$$

$$= 9\,000 \text{ cycles to failure.}$$

What we have calculated is a very very crude approximation to the observed phenomenon of metal fatigue, i.e. failure under the repeated application of a stress which is smaller than the normal fracture stress. In real solids, the process is vastly more complex, but there is a grain of truth in this model. Dislocations moving under stress concentrated by cracks can cause the cracks to grow.

You should have succeeded with part 1 of this question without great difficulty, but if you managed the second part too you may polish your halo a bit!

SAQ 10

The resolved shear stress in the plane is

$$= \sigma \sin 60° \cos 60°$$

$$= \sigma\sqrt{3/4} = 0.433$$

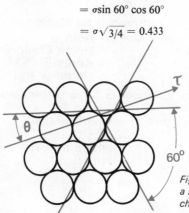

Figure 43 The three glide channels and a shear stress τ at angle θ to one channel.

The resolved component of this shear stress along the sliding channel most nearly aligned with σ is $\sigma \cos \theta$ (see Fig. 43). The largest possible value of θ is 30° (if $\theta > 39°$ another channel will have $\theta < 30°$) so the minimum component of the shear stress is $\sigma\sqrt{3/4} \cos 30°$

$$= \sigma\sqrt{3/4} \cdot \sqrt{3/2} = 3/8\,\sigma = 0.375\,\sigma$$

SAQ 11
The answer to SAQ 11 is Figure 44 (p. 46).

SAQ 12
You should have made the following points:

1 The stress needed to displace the dislocation depends upon the rate of change of the total potential energy with position of the atoms in the dislocated region of the crystal.

2 The fluctuations of potential energy as the dislocation moves are the result of small changes in the potential energy sum consequent upon small changes in the complex geometry around the dislocation.

3 The pair-potential functions are not known with sufficient accuracy to allow useful calculations of the fluctuations of potential energy.

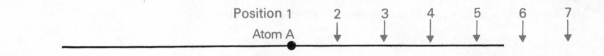

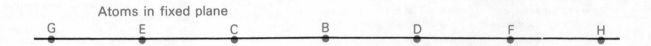

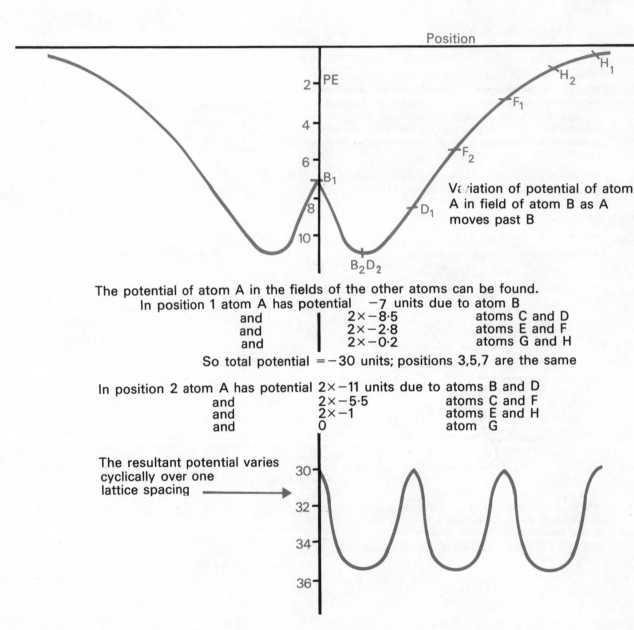

Variation of potential of atom A in field of atom B as A moves past B

The potential of atom A in the fields of the other atoms can be found.
In position 1 atom A has potential   −7 units due to atom B
and   2×−8·5   atoms C and D
and   2×−2·8   atoms E and F
and   2×−0·2   atoms G and H

So total potential =−30 units; positions 3,5,7 are the same

In position 2 atom A has potential 2×−11 units due to atoms B and D
and   2×−5·5   atoms C and F
and   2×−1   atoms E and H
and   0   atom G

The resultant potential varies cyclically over one lattice spacing →

Figure 44

Unit 8 Thermal Properties of Solids

Contents

Table A

List of scientific terms, concepts and principles used in Unit 8

Introduced in a previous Unit or a Foundation Course	Course and Unit No.	Introduced in this Unit	Page No.
Hooke's law	S100/22*; T100/9**	method of mixtures	5
Young modulus	S100/22; T100/9	Dulong-Petit law	7
fundamentai	S100/30	restoring force	7
overtones	S100/30	simple harmonic motion	8
Boltzmann function	S100/5; ST28-/2	period	8
specific heat	ST28-/2	force constant	8
activation energy	S100/11; ST28-/5	Einstein frequency	10
Planck constant	S100/29	elastic waves	13
		phonons	14
		anharmonic oscillator	21
		Grüneisen's law	22
		Lindemann's law of melting	23
		point defects	26
		vacancy	27
		interstitial	27
		impurity atom	27
		random walk	30

* The Open University (1971) S100 *Science: A Foundation Course,* The Open University Press.

** The Open University (1972) T100 *The Man-made World: A Foundation Course,* The Open University Press.

Aims

The aims of this Unit are:

(i) to describe the ways in which a solid is affected by heat;

(ii) to show that these effects are a consequence of the average kinetic energy per atom increasing with temperature;

(iii) to use a mechanical analogue to show that thermal properties arise from atomic vibrations about lattice sites.

Objectives

When you have completed this Unit you should be able to:

1 Define, or recognize adequate definitions of, the terms listed in Table A.

2 Describe an experimental method for determining the specific heat capacity of a solid.

3 State the principles of the Dulong-Petit law.

4 Describe qualitatively the need for the Einstein model.

5 Explain thermal expansion and melting in terms of a potential-energy curve.

6 Describe qualitatively the process by which a solid conducts heat.

7 List the most important types of point defects in solids.

8 Explain the effect of temperature on the density of defects in a solid.

9 Describe diffusion in a solid qualitatively in terms of the random walk of defects.

10 Describe at least two uses of diffusion in technology.

11 Discuss the usefulness of a mechanical model in understanding the thermal properties of solids.

Study Guide

This Unit describes an area of experimental science—the thermal properties of solids—and accordingly it has a heavy experimental component. The experiments are all short, however, so I hope you will not find them a burden. Most of the experiments are vital to the development of the ideas in the Unit, so you should try to make time for them. You will find it very useful to get out the equipment for all the experiments before you study the Unit, so that you will have it on hand when needed. Unless you have plenty of spare time, try not to spend longer on the experiments than I have suggested—they are all intended to give you a general 'feel' for the subject, rather than be rigorous measurements. If you approach them in this spirit, you will find they make a valuable contribution to your understanding of the Unit.

As the television programme associated with this Unit deals with diffusion processes in solids, gases and liquids, you will find it very helpful to have read Sections 8.5 and 8.6 and completed Experiment 8.6 before seeing the TV component. Even if you have not studied the Unit at all by the TV date, try at least to read quickly through these Sections. You will find the TV much more useful as a result.

Otherwise the study sequence of this Unit is perfectly simple. Proceed sequentially through the Unit, doing the Experiments and SAQs as they arise.

8.1   Introduction

This Unit looks at another aspect of the role of kinetic energy in determining the behaviour of atoms. Unit 7 discussed the basic structure of solids, and this Unit looks at the way solids behave when the average kinetic energy of the atoms is increased by raising the temperature. Consideration of the way an atom might utilize this kinetic energy leads to a mechanical model for the atom in a solid. The model is a very powerful one, and with only minor modifications provides an explanation for a variety of phenomena: heat capacity, thermal expansion, melting and diffusion in solids. The final Sections of the Unit examine the defects which are produced in a lattice by heating and their importance in the diffusion of atoms. The technological significance of being able to persuade atoms in a solid to move around is considerable, so applications of diffusion are also discussed.

8.2   Heat capacity of a solid

In this Section we shall examine the heat capacity of a solid, beginning with experimental work on this subject. The explanation of heat capacity put forward by Dulong and Petit will be discussed, as this was the first significant generalization of experimental data in the field. Further experiments showed their approach to have some serious deficiencies, which will be examined. Your knowledge of the nature of solids (Unit 7), interatomic forces (Unit 2) and Newtonian mechanics (Unit 1) will then be used to set up a model of the atom in a solid, leading to a better explanation of heat capacity. The same model will be used in later Sections of the Unit to account for other thermal properties of solids.

8.2.1   Heat and temperature

When heat is supplied to an object, its temperature usually increases. The quantity of heat needed to raise the temperature of a given object by 1 K defines the *total heat capacity* of that object.

total heat capacity

In what units would you expect a total heat capacity to be expressed?

Since it is a quantity of heat per unit of temperature increase, it is expressed in $J K^{-1}$.

Think about the heating of objects in everyday life. What factors will determine the heat capacity of an object?

Your experience probably suggests that the mass of the object and the material from which it is made affect the heat capacity.

How could you determine the heat capacity of an object experimentally?

Clearly, it is necessary to supply a known quantity of heat to the object and determine the change in temperature.

You may recall that Joule's experiments which established the equivalence between heat and work took this form. A known amount of energy was dissipated into an insulated beaker of water, and its temperature was measured. There are some obvious difficulties in applying this method to solids—how do you rotate paddles in a lump of metal? That problem may be overcome by supplying electrical energy rather than mechanical—for example, one could pass a measured current through the piece of metal and observe its temperature change. To calculate the heat capacity of the solid, we need to know the absolute value of the energy supplied, and so our knowledge of the heat capacity can only be as precise as that measurement. It is more usual to determine heat capacities by comparison, using the *method of mixtures*—a technique which should be familiar to you if you have studied T100.

method of mixtures

SAQ 1   1 kg of water at 10 °C is mixed with 1 kg of water at 30 °C. Assuming no heat is lost, what will be the final temperature of the mixture?

ANSWER I hope it is obvious that the final temperature of the mixture will be 20 °C, since the heat given up by the kilogram of hot water in cooling by 10 °C will be just enough to warm the cold water by the same amount*.

This simple example illustrates a general principle, which may be used to analyse more complex situations. If two objects at different temperatures are placed in contact, heat will flow from the hotter one to the cooler one until they reach the same temperature. If there are no heat losses to the surroundings, the amount of heat gained by the cold body will be equal to the amount of heat lost by the hot body. This principle makes it possible to calculate the final temperature of a mixture from information about its components.

SAQ 2   If 3 kg of water at 10 °C is mixed with 1 kg of water at 30 °C, and no heat is lost, what will be the final temperature of the mixture?

ANSWER   We know that heat lost = heat gained. Assume that 3 kg of water has three times the heat capacity of 1 kg of water, and that the mixture reaches a final temperature of T °C.

Then heat lost by hot water $= (30 - T)$ units.
Heat gained by cold water $= 3(T - 10)$ units.

$$3(T - 10) = 30 - T$$
$$3T - 30 = 30 - T$$
$$4T = 60$$
so $$T = 15$$

The mixture's temperature is 15 °C.

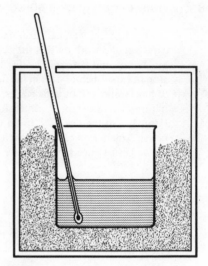

Figure 1   Cross-section of a typical calorimeter.

calorimeter

The two examples we have considered were mixtures of a single material. Life is not usually so simple. Even if we wanted to do a simple experiment mixing two samples of water, they would be placed in a container of some kind. Clearly equilibrium is only reached when the mixture and the container reach the same temperature. Calculating this temperature requires a knowledge of the respective heat capacities of the water and the container. Conversely, measuring initial and final temperatures makes it possible to calculate the heat capacity of the container, assuming that we know the heat capacity of the water. We can use water to calibrate our system. Heat capacities are normally determined by use of a *calorimeter*, which typically consists of a metal can inside a wooden box packed with insulating material. The box is normally covered to prevent heat being convected away, with a small slot to allow a thermometer to be placed inside. The diagram of a typical calorimeter (Fig. 1) illustrates its layout. The insulation is intended to reduce loss of heat to the surroundings, since this would be a source of error. The beaker is usually made of some material with a low heat capacity, such as copper. The outer container is usually wood. Quite respectable calorimetry can, however, be done with much simpler apparatus, such as that supplied in your Home Kit. You should do Home Experiment 8.1 at this stage, particularly if you have no recent experience of measuring heat capacities.

Did your simple experiment confirm your everyday experience of heat capacity?

I hope you observed that the heat capacity of an object was dependent on its mass and the material from which it was made.

specific heat capacity
molar heat capacity

Obviously, it would be tedious to measure the heat capacity of any object being considered for an application in which this property is relevant. It is more usual to calculate the heat capacity of an object from its mass and such properties of the material as either *specific heat capacity*, which is heat capacity per unit mass, or *molar heat capacity*—heat capacity per mole of the material. Dulong and Petit calculated the molar heat capacities of several elements from calorimetric data (in 1819!) and made a surprising discovery. Look at this table:

* This assumes that the heat capacity of water is independent of temperature. While such an assumption is permissible for a rough calculation of this type, we shall see later that the heat capacity of an object depends on temperature.

6

Substance	Molar heat capacity (J mol^{-1} K^{-1})
Sodium	28.5
Aluminium	24.7
Sulphur	23.4
Copper	24.6
Silver	25.4
Tin	26.7
Lead	26.0

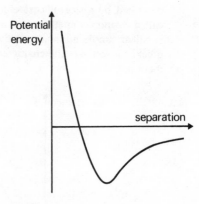

Figure 2

What do you notice? The table includes some soft metals, some hard metals, even a non-metal: in every case the molar heat capacity is about 25 J mol^{-1} K^{-1}. The observation that molar heat capacity is approximately the same for many solids is known as the Dulong-Petit law. This result is, at first sight, a little surprising. You know that materials differ widely in their heat capacities—why should sulphur have almost the same heat capacity per mole as aluminium? To answer this question, we need to look more closely at the way atoms join together to form a solid.

8.2.2 Atoms in solids

Unit 7 described the conditions necessary for atoms to form a solid, and the importance of the curve of potential energy against atomic separation in determining the parameters of the solid. What fundamental property of the solid is exhibited by the curve (Fig. 2)?

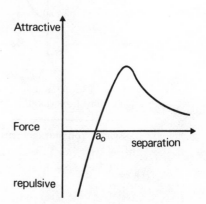

Figure 3

The equilibrium separation between atoms in the solid is at the distinct minimum of this curve. Remember how this curve arises, by combining the results of the attraction between distant atoms and the repulsion at short range. If atoms approach each other so that their separation becomes less than the equilibrium value, they will tend to move further apart—if you also recall the force-separation curve (Fig. 3), a repulsive force tends to move them apart. In contrast, if an atom drifts away from its neighbour, so that their separation becomes greater than a_0, an attractive force makes it tend to move back. So the atom is constrained always to move back towards an equilibrium position. Can you think of a mechanical system similar to the atom in a solid? Consider a mass on the end of a stretched spring, as in Figure 4. If it is lifted up, it tends to fall back towards the equilibrium position. Similarly, if the mass is pulled down the spring will exert a force tending to restore the original situation. There is at least a superficial similarity between the forces acting on such a mass and those acting on an atom: displacement leads to a *restoring force*, which tends to get things back into the equilibrium position.

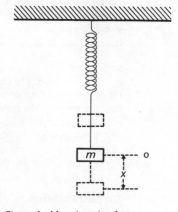

Figure 4 Mass hanging from a stretched spring.

SAQ 3 Describe the transfer of energy in such a system.

ANSWER As you probably remember from Unit 1, when a spring is stretched it is given stored energy or *potential energy*. When the spring is released, the energy is used to accelerate the mass, which thereby acquires *kinetic energy*. Can you think of another common mechanical system where this process of energy transfer also occurs?

The simple pendulum is another example of a system where potential energy (gravitational potential energy, in this case) is converted to kinetic energy when the bob is released.

What happens to the kinetic energy of the moving pendulum?

It does work, lifting the bob and giving it gravitational potential energy.

In both these examples—the pendulum and the mass on a spring—the displaced massive particle oscillates about its equilibrium position. Both vibrations are examples of a particular type of motion, described in the supplement to Unit 1*,

* The Open University (1973) *Elements of Dynamics: A Revision Text (ED)*, The Open University Press.

This type of vibration is called *simple harmonic motion*. In general, if a particle oscillates about its equilibrium position under the influence of a force that is always proportional to the displacement from equilibrium, the motion is said to be simple harmonic. The term arises from the observation that the displacement from equilibrium of such a particle varies with time in a way which may be described by a sine or cosine curve (Fig. 5). Sines and cosines are sometimes called harmonic functions, and motion which may be described in terms of them is called simple harmonic motion or, more usually, S.H.M. You should now quickly investigate the characteristics of such motion by doing Home Experiment 8.2.

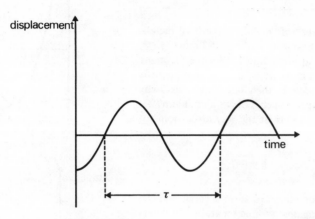

Figure 5

SAQ 4   Did the results of the experiment confirm the expressions obtained in Unit 1 for a mass vibrating on a stretched spring?

ANSWER   You probably remember that the expression obtained in *ED*, Section S1.3.3 was

$$\tau = 2\pi \sqrt{\frac{m}{k}}$$

where the period of oscillation, τ, was given in terms of the mass of the bob, m, and the force constant of the spring, k^*. This expression suggests that the period should vary as the square root of the mass of the bob, and be substantially independent of the amplitude of vibration. I hope your experimental results are in agreement!

SAQ 5   An object of mass 0.2 kg is attached to a vertical spring, which extends by 5 cm as a result. The object is removed and replaced by one having a mass of 1.0 kg, which is then pulled down below its equilibrium position and released. Find the period of the resulting S.H.M.

ANSWER   The force constant, f, is defined as the force per unit displacement, so

$$f = \frac{0.2 \times 9.8}{0.05} \text{ N m}^{-1} \ (= \text{kg s}^{-2})$$

The period of vibration is given by

$$\tau = 2\pi \sqrt{m/f}$$

$$= 2\pi \sqrt{\frac{0.05}{0.2 \times 9.8}}$$

$$\approx 1.0 \text{ s}$$

Another important way of describing the characteristic vibration of an oscillator is by expressing its *frequency*. This is simply the number of times each second that the mass passes a particular point moving in one fixed direction. Since the period

* To avoid confusion with the Boltzmann constant, k, which we shall be using later in this Unit, we shall use f to denote the force constant.

8

is the time it takes the mass to return to a particular point in its regular cycle, the frequency is simply the inverse of the period.

$$\text{Period } \tau = 2\pi \sqrt{\frac{m}{f}} \quad \text{s}$$

$$\text{Frequency } \nu = \frac{1}{2\pi} \sqrt{\frac{f}{m}} \quad \text{s}^{-1}$$

SAQ 6   What is the frequency of vibration of the mass in SAQ 10?

ANSWER   1.0 hertz (vibrations per second).

I hope you have not lost sight of our goal, in exploring the properties of systems where a force tends to constrain a mass towards an equilibrium position. We were seeking a mechanical analogue to the position of an atom in a solid, constrained by interatomic forces. If we represent the forces between atoms by mechanical springs, we can visualize an atom at its equilibrium position in a simple cubic lattice (Fig. 6). This model is in accord with the graph of interatomic force against distance—for the region near equilibrium, the force tending to restore the atom is proportional to its displacement from equilibrium. In terms of Figure 6, if the atom is given a small push along the direction of one pair of springs, it will exhibit S.H.M. along that line, since the springs in the other two directions will be virtually unchanged in length. But, for the atom to vibrate, it must acquire kinetic energy, just as the spring or pendulum does. The pendulum and the mass on a stretched spring require human intervention to gain kinetic energy: how does the atom gain enough energy to move in a solid?

You may remember that Unit 3, Section 3.3.3 discussed a working definition of temperature, concluding that temperature could be defined in terms of the mean kinetic energy of atoms. The expression finally derived in that Section was $T = 2/3k \, (\tfrac{1}{2} m \, \bar{u}^2)$ where T is the temperature, k is the Boltzmann constant and $(\tfrac{1}{2} m \, \bar{u}^2)$ is the mean kinetic energy per atom. Since this working definition gives the temperature as a function of the mean kinetic energy, we can use it to express the mean kinetic energy in terms of the temperature.

$$\text{Mean kinetic energy} = \tfrac{1}{2} m \, \bar{u}^2 = \frac{3}{2} k \, T.$$

For an atom in a three-dimensional solid, there are three degrees of freedom for movement (Fig. 6), so we can suggest that this energy is evenly shared between them (nature has no preferred direction!). This brings us to the conclusion that the atoms in a solid have average kinetic energies of $\tfrac{1}{2}kT$ for each degree of freedom. Since each atom is confined between its nearest neighbours by interatomic forces, we could perhaps argue that the kinetic energy would be manifested in atomic vibrations. How could a theory like this be tested?

The obvious thing to do is calculate the vibration frequency which would result if the atom behaved like a mechanical oscillator, and see if the result is physically sensible.

What is the expression for vibration frequency of a mechanical oscillator? How could the terms in this expression be evaluated for an atom in a solid?

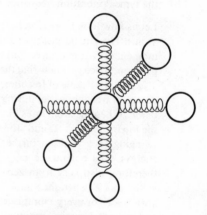

Figure 6   An atom in its equilibrium position.

Frequency $\nu = 1/2\pi \, \sqrt{f/m}$. To determine the frequency of vibration for an atom in a solid therefore requires a knowledge of the atomic mass (m) and the force constant (f). The atomic mass is easily determined by dividing the molar mass by the Avogadro number. Force per unit displacement can be obtained from tabulated values of the Young modulus—the ratio of percentage elongation of a solid (strain) to the applied stress (force per unit area). The force constant, remember, was defined as force per unit displacement.

If a force F is applied to a length l of a solid having cross-sectional area A, the ratio of the extension resulting (e) to the applied force may be written in terms of the Young modulus E as:

$$\frac{F}{e} = \frac{AE}{l} \qquad \left(\text{since } E = \frac{F/A}{e/l} = \frac{F \cdot l}{e \cdot A.}\right)$$

Consider now a cube of edge a_0, the average spacing between atoms. Its length is a_0 and its cross-sectional area a_0^2, so the extension Δa produced by a force F is given by:

$$\frac{F}{\Delta a} = \frac{a_0^2 E}{a_0} = a_0 \, E.$$

This gives us a value for f, since it is force per unit displacement.

$$\therefore f = \frac{F}{\Delta a} = a_0 E.$$

9

SAQ 7 Using the following data, calculate the vibrational frequency for atoms in aluminium. ($E = 7.1 \cdot 10^{10}$ Nm^{-2}; $a_0 = 2.84 \cdot 10^{-10}$ m; atomic weight = 27 g mol^{-1}).

ANSWER $f = a_0 E = 2.84 \cdot 10^{-10}$ m $\times$ $7.1 \cdot 10^{10}$ Nm^{-2}

$$= 20.1 \text{ Nm}^{-1}$$

$$m = \frac{2.7 \cdot 10^{-2}}{6.02 \cdot 10^{23}} \text{ kg}$$

$$= 4.48 \cdot 10^{-26} \text{ kg}$$

$$\nu = \frac{1}{2\pi} \sqrt{\frac{f}{m}} \quad \text{s}^{-1}$$

$$= 0.16 \sqrt{\frac{20.1}{4.48 \cdot 10^{-26}}} \text{ s}^{-1}$$

$$= 0.16 \sqrt{4.50 \cdot 10^{26}} \text{ s}^{-1}$$

$$= 0.16 \times 2.13 \cdot 10^{13} \text{ s}^{-1}$$

$$= 3.4 \cdot 10^{12} \text{ s}^{-1}$$

So, our calculations indicate that atoms in a metal vibrate back and forth more than 10^{12} times each second—in fact, more refined estimates put typical values of ν closer to 10^{13} hertz. This fundamental vibration rate for an atom in a solid is known as the *Einstein frequency*, because the great physicist Albert Einstein advanced this model as a solution for the unexpected behaviour of the heat capacity of solids at low temperature. The Einstein model is discussed in more detail in Section 8.2.5. The important principle to grasp at this stage is that atoms in a solid exhibit their thermal energy in vibrations, and an approximate value of the typical vibration frequency may be obtained from a mechanical analogue.

Einstein frequency

Let us now look more closely at the total energy in a solid composed of vibrating atoms. The kinetic energy of a particle describing S.H.M. varies from zero (at the moment of changing direction) to a maximum as it passes through the equilibrium position. Since we know that the average kinetic energy of an atom at temperature T is $\frac{1}{2}kT$ per degree of freedom, it follows that the kinetic energy of the atom per degree of freedom varies during the cycle from a minimum of zero to a maximum of kT. When the atom loses kinetic energy by slowing down, it does work against the interatomic forces and stores potential energy (just as the moving pendulum, swinging to a position further from the centre of the Earth, stores potential energy). The potential energy stored per degree of vibrational freedom must, therefore, also vary from zero (when the kinetic energy reaches its maximum value) to kT (when the kinetic energy is zero). The total energy of the system is always kT for every vibrational direction, with the distribution between kinetic and potential energy continually altering.

Consider now a mole of a substance, containing N_A identical atoms. Each atom has, on average, $3\,kT$ of thermal energy—kT for each vibrational direction. The mole of material, therefore, has a total thermal energy of $3\,N_A\,kT$ J. If the substance is heated and the volume is kept constant, all the heat supplied will go into increasing the energy of the atomic oscillators. Since the total energy at temperature T is equal to $3\,N_A\,kT$ joule, it follows that the increase in energy for every kelvin rise in temperature is $3\,N_A\,k$ J. The molar heat capacity at constant volume for any substance described by this model should, therefore, be $3\,N_A\,k$ J mol^{-1} K^{-1}.

SAQ 8 Calculate the numerical value of the molar heat capacity predicted by this expression.

ANSWER $C_{V,m} = 3\,N_A\,k$ J mol^{-1} K^{-1}

$$= 3 \times 6.022 \cdot 10^{23} \times 1.380 \cdot 10^{-23} \text{ J mol}^{-1} \text{ K}^{-1}$$

$$= 24.9 \text{ J mol}^{-1} \text{ K}^{-1}$$

Does this number ring a bell?

I hope it does—we started this Section hoping to explain why a whole range of substances proved to have molar heat capacities around 25 J mol^{-1} K^{-1}.

Setting up a model of the atom in a solid as a vibrating particle, constrained by interatomic forces to describe S.H.M., leads to an explanation for the Dulong-Petit law. At the very least, this suggests that the model is worth further exploration.

SAQ 9 (Revision)   You probably remember (from Section 3.4.2) that the molar heat capacity of a perfect gas is $(3/2)N_A k$ J mol^{-1} K^{-1}. Why does the solid composed of atomic oscillators have a heat capacity exactly twice that of a gas?

ANSWER   The atoms in a gas have only kinetic energy; those in a solid can also store energy as potential energy, so they have twice as many degrees of freedom (i.e. 6).

8.2.3   Interaction of vibrating systems

The model developed in Section 8.2.3 appears to give useful agreement with experimental values for heat capacity. It may have occurred to you, however, that there is one somewhat naïve aspect of our model. We have assumed that the force restoring an atom to its equilibrium position will always be proportional to the atom's displacement. This implies that we regard the atom as vibrating in the space between other atoms which are fixed in position. Why is this a naïve model?

Clearly the atom we have chosen is not in any way 'special', so if it is vibrating as a result of having thermal energy, all the other atoms in the solid will also be vibrating. We should investigate the likely amplitude of these atomic vibrations, since obviously the neighbouring atoms may only be regarded as 'fixed' if their oscillations have amplitudes much smaller than the interatomic spacing. Let us look more closely at the characteristics of our mechanical model, which were set up in *ED* (Section S1.3.3). The treatment used in that Unit sets up a simple mathematical representation of the vibrating system in terms of simple sinusoidal curves. Earlier in this Unit (Fig. 5) we graphed the displacement of a particle exhibiting S.H.M. against time, in accordance with the expression from Unit 1: for motion along the x-axis, the displacement varies with time according to $x = x_0 \cos(\sqrt{f/m}\,(t))$. This expression can be differentiated to give the velocity $(\mathrm{d}x/\mathrm{d}t)$ and the acceleration $(\mathrm{d}^2x/\mathrm{d}t^2)$. These also vary sinusoidally, as shown in Figure 7. The expressions for velocity and acceleration also contain the amplitude of vibration, x_0. We will now use these to compute a value for x_0.

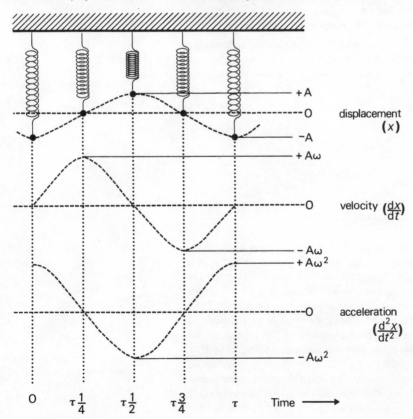

Figure 7   Relationship between displacement, velocity and acceleration in S.H.M.

11

SAQ 10   How can we use one of these expressions to solve for the amplitude of vibration of an atom?

ANSWER   One way is to use our knowledge of the maximum kinetic energy per atom (kT for each direction of vibration). We can obtain the kinetic energy of the atom at maximum velocity, equate this to kT and solve, using the techniques developed in Unit 1.

$$\text{Kinetic energy} = \tfrac{1}{2}mv^2$$

$$\text{Maximum kinetic energy} = \tfrac{1}{2}mv^2_{\max}$$

Now
$$v = \frac{\mathrm{d}x}{\mathrm{d}t} = \frac{\mathrm{d}}{\mathrm{d}t}\left(x_0 \cos\sqrt{\frac{f}{m}}\cdot t\right)$$

$$= x_0 \cdot \sqrt{\frac{f}{m}} \cdot \sin\sqrt{\frac{f}{m}} \cdot t$$

This function will be a maximum when $\sin\sqrt{f/m}\cdot t = 1$, so the maximum velocity is:

$$v_{\max} = x_0 \cdot \sqrt{\frac{f}{m}}$$

So the maximum K.E. $= \tfrac{1}{2}\,m\,v^2_{\max}$

$$= \tfrac{1}{2}\,m\left(x_0\sqrt{\frac{f}{m}}\right)^2$$

$$= \tfrac{1}{2}\,m \cdot \frac{f}{m} \cdot x_0^2$$

$$= \tfrac{1}{2}\,f\,x_0^2$$

Equating with the known maximum K.E.,

$$\tfrac{1}{2}f x_0^2 = kT$$

So
$$x_0^2 = \frac{2kT}{f}$$

And hence
$$x_0 = \sqrt{\frac{2kT}{f}}$$

This means that the amplitude of atomic vibrations can be calculated simply from the force constant and the temperature.

SAQ 11   From the data previously used (SAQ 7) for aluminium, calculate the amplitude of atomic vibrations at room temperature ($T = 300$ K, say).

ANSWER $x_0 = \sqrt{\dfrac{2kT}{f}}$

$$= \sqrt{\frac{2 \cdot 1.38 \cdot 10^{-23} \cdot 300}{20.1}}\ \text{m}.$$

$$= \sqrt{4.14 \cdot 10^{-22}}\ \text{m}$$

$$\approx 2.0 \cdot 10^{-11}\ \text{m}$$

Thus the amplitude of atomic vibrations at room temperature is about one-fourteenth of the interatomic spacing ($a_0 = 2.84 \times 10^{-10}$ m). Once again you will probably be pleasantly surprised to learn that the prediction from our simple model is in good agreement with experiments—in this case, X-ray diffraction studies. It is also important to note that our model predicts that the amplitude of atomic vibrations will increase as the temperature goes up. The implications of this increase as the temperature goes up. The implications of this prediction are considered later in this Unit (Section 8.3.3). For the moment, we will leave that question, since our purpose in calculating a typical vibration amplitude was to decide whether atomic oscillators might interact. Because the vibrations represent a significant fraction of the interatomic distance, even at room temperature, it seems quite likely that the vibrations of an atom will perturb its neighbours. One way of investigating this interaction would be to extend our mechanical model by coupling together two or more vibrating systems, as you did in the Home Experiment for Unit 6. What did this experiment show?

There was an interaction between the linked systems and energy was transferred from one to the next. Indeed, the experiment could be extended to show that energy supplied at one end of a row of oscillators might be transferred right along to the other end. Such a process in a solid can be visualized if we extend our mechanical model, in which the forces between an atom and its neighbours are seen as being analogous to springs. Imagine a whole solid on these lines, with each particle connected to its neighbours by springs, as in Figure 8. Energy can be transferred from one vibrating particle to the next, and so it passes along the solid. As the 'springs' are deformed in just the same way as they are when the solid is stretched or compressed by a small amount, transfer of energy in a solid by this means is usually called an *elastic wave*.

elastic wave

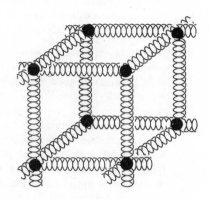

For example, if a metal rod is struck at one end, the atoms at that end are forced closer to their neighbours. Repulsive forces, analogous to our springs, cause the neighbours to move away and hence closer to the next layer of atoms—and so a wave of compression travels through the solid. If the method of transmission of energy is really the interaction of vibrations, we should be able to predict the velocity of an elastic wave in a solid. Consider an atom at the end of a metal rod, and think of it as being (for the sake of argument) at rest before it is acted on by an exterior force, e.g. a hammer below. How long after the energy is applied with the atom transfer the energy to its neighbour?

The time lag will be one-quarter of the atom's vibration period—if you look back to Figure 7, the time difference between zero displacement and the maximum value is $\tau/4$.

Figure 8 *Mechanical analogue of a solid.*

SAQ 12 Assuming that the period of vibration of atoms in a brass rod is 10^{-13} seconds and that the average interatomic distance is $1.30 \cdot 10^{-10}$ m, calculate the speed of an elastic wave in a brass rod.

ANSWER The wave will progress one interatomic distance every quarter of the vibration period, so its velocity may be obtained by dividing a_0 ($1.30 \cdot 10^{-10}$ m) by $\frac{1}{4}\tau$ ($2.5 \cdot 10^{-14}$ seconds).

$$v = \frac{a_0}{\frac{1}{4}\tau}$$

$$\approx \frac{1.30 \cdot 10^{-10}}{2.5 \cdot 10^{-14}}$$

$$\approx 5\,000 \text{ m s}^{-1}$$

This calculation gives a very high speed for the wave of compression. It assumed that the atoms were at rest—how valid is that assumption?

Clearly the atoms are not at rest, since our model is one of vibrating atoms. The atoms will, however, be found on average to have separations of atoms at rest if any solid of real size is considered, since any one atom is as likely to be one side of the equilibrium position as the other. As even a millimetre of brass contains 8 000 000 atomic distances, averaging is quite allowable!

Perhaps you are wondering if this prediction of very high speeds for elastic waves in solids is borne out by experiment. Obviously, it would be possible to strike one end of a metal rod and measure the time interval before the wave of compression reached the other end, but this would involve measuring very small periods of time for any reasonable length of rod (if the theory is even remotely near to being correct). Let us consider, however, what will happen when the wave reaches the far end of the rod. The last atom in the chain will be displaced from its equilibrium position by the energy supplied, but unless this energy is sufficient to dislodge the atom completely from the solid it will be drawn back (by the attractive force) towards its neighbour. It will then cause the neighbouring atom to move, and so the wave will effectively have been reflected. The pulse could travel back and forth within the rod for some time, until its energy is dissipated and it dies out. How could you detect this behaviour?

When a wave of compression reaches the atoms at the end of the rod, they will be displaced and compress the air in the immediate vicinity. This will happen every time the wave reaches that end, so the air in that region will be periodically compressed. This periodic compression is, of course, a sound wave, so you could possibly detect the wave's travel back and forth along the rod by ear! What will determine the pitch of the sound?

The pitch of a sound is its frequency, or the number of disturbances per second. Clearly, in this case, the number of disturbances per second is given by the number of times each second that the wave makes a round trip—to the other end of the rod and back. If the length of the rod is known, the number of round trips per second gives the velocity of the wave.

Velocity = (number of round trips per second) × (distance of round trip).

Thus, if the rod is l metres long and the sound has frequency f, the velocity v is given by:

$$v = 2lf \ \text{m s}^{-1}$$

Home Experiment 8.3 is a simple attempt to test whether the velocity of sound in brass agrees with the value predicted from our mechanical analogue (SAQ 12). You should do the experiment now—it will take you about ten minutes.

I hope the experiment convinced you that the estimate of the velocity of elastic waves was quite a fair one—when I did the experiment on the Home Kit proto-type, I found very good agreement with our prediction. It is staggering how much more rapidly a sound vibration travels in a solid than it does in the air. If you have studied S100, you will probably have recognized the compressional wave as the P-wave generated by the seismic disturbance. A wave of compression travelling through a solid behaves in many ways as if it were a particle, so such waves are often referred to as *phonons*. Their behaviour is an advanced study, lying beyond the scope of this Course. They do have one property which is very important for our investigation of a model for atoms in a solid. For any given solid, pulses of this type essentially have a fixed velocity—you probably noticed while doing Home Experiment 8.3 that the frequency of the sound wave produced was not dependent on how firmly you struck the rod. More importantly, experi-ments which are more precise than the one you performed confirm the validity of predictions based on our model of interacting atomic oscillators.

phonons

SAQ 13   Why is sound transmitted much more rapidly in solids than in gases, when the average kinetic energy per atom is determined by the temperature for both cases?

ANSWER   In a solid, the vibrating atoms are strongly coupled, and so displacement of one atom causes its neighbours to move. In a gas, on the other hand, the atoms are randomly positioned and move with random directions. As a result, supplying energy to one atom does not necessarily have any effect on an immedi-ate neighbour—the energetic atom can move off in any direction.

8.2.4   Some restrictions on energy

We have experienced considerable success so far in the analysis of the thermal properties of solids by reference to a mechanical analogy. There is yet another property of vibrating mechanical systems which we should now incorporate—a restriction on the type of vibrations allowed. If you have studied S100, you will probably find this quite familiar territory.

Presumably, one of our primitive ancestors noticed that the twang of a bow-string can be pleasant to the ear, and constructed the forerunner of a legion of musical instruments which rely on the same principle: if a string of some sort is stretched and then plucked, it vibrates. The string may be of wire or of catgut; it may be stimulated by bowing, plucking or striking; the result may be tuneful or agonizing; in all cases, however, the same physical principles apply. How, then, might the great differences in sound when the same note is played on different stringed instruments be explained? Middle C on a piano has the same basic *frequency* as middle C on a guitar or a violin, yet they sound quite different. This is because the plucking of a string does not generate a single vibration, but a complex pattern containing several frequencies. If the pattern is analysed care-fully, it becomes apparent that the vibrations present all have frequencies which are exact integral multiples of the *fundamental* frequency of the string. These

fundamental

14

higher frequencies are called *overtones* by musicians, but we will refer to them as higher harmonics. If the fundamental vibration frequency of the string is v, the higher harmonics will have frequencies $2v, 3v, 4v$ . . . and be called respectively the second, third, fourth . . . harmonics. There is a basic physical reason why only certain vibration frequencies are possible on any given stretched string. Since the two ends are fixed, the string can only vibrate in ways which allow no movement of these two points. If stimulated by a mechanical vibrator, a string will respond to frequencies which satisfy this condition—as the frequency is gradually increased, the vibrations shown in Figure 9 will occur*.

overtones

v

$2v$

$3v$

$4v$

Figure 9   Vibrations of frequencies v, $2v$, $3v$ and $4v$ on a stretched string.

It turns out that the frequencies allowed are integral multiples of the fundamental frequency. Exactly which of these harmonics will appear, and their relative intensities, characterize the sound of a particular instrument. The physical dimensions of the system place restrictions on the modes of vibration.

In our discussion of atomic vibrations, we have assumed so far that the total energy of any atomic oscillator can have any value (subject, of course, to the average energy per degree of freedom for all the atoms being $\frac{1}{2}kT$ at temperature T). There is, however, an additional restriction on possible energies. Just as a string vibrates only at discrete frequencies, separated in frequency by v, so an atomic oscillator is also only able to have discrete values of energy, separated in energy by hv (where h is the Planck constant). If an atomic oscillator could be cooled to the absolute zero of temperature, it would still have a vibrational energy of $\frac{1}{2}hv$—this is known as the zero-point energy. At higher temperatures, the oscillator may have one of the higher permitted values of energy, which are given by $(n + \frac{1}{2}) hv$ for n an integer; in other words, its vibration may have one of a set of larger possible amplitudes for the same frequency.

SAQ 14   Calculate the separation between allowed values of energy for an atom with vibrational frequency

$$v = 5 \cdot 10^{12} \text{ s}^{-1}. \text{ (Use } h \approx 6.6 \cdot 10^{-34} \text{ J s.)}$$

ANSWER   Separation $= hv$

$= 6.6 \times 10^{-34} \times 5 \times 10^{12}$ J

$\approx 3 \cdot 10^{-21}$ J.

The energy gap between allowed values is very small indeed—if you calculate its size for real mechanical devices it will be very obvious why this limitation does not manifest itself in pendulum clocks!

What is the gap between allowed energies for a pendulum which vibrates once each second?

* If you studied S100, you will recognize that the frequencies permitted are those for which the length of the string is an integral number of half-wavelengths.

The gap will be 10^{-34} joule, compared with a typical total energy of at least 10^{-6} joule—in other words, the steps in the energy 'staircase' are so tiny that it becomes effectively a ramp, and any value of energy is permitted. Similarly, when atoms are at relatively high temperatures, the gaps between allowed energies are not readily discernible. The limitation becomes significant when the temperature is lowered. How would you go about predicting the temperature below which this 'quantization' of energy (as it is usually called) becomes significant?

Since you know the step between allowed energies is $h\nu$, and the average total energy per vibration is kT, you possibly guessed that the effect becomes important when these are of about the same size. This is what is observed in practice, as will be discussed in Section 8.2.5.

SAQ 15   The temperature T at which $h\nu = kT$ is known as the *Einstein temperature* for the substance concerned. Calculate the Einstein temperature for the material whose data was given in SAQ 14.

ANSWER   At the Einstein temperature, $h\nu = kT$ and therefore

$$T = \frac{h\nu}{k}$$

For the substance concerned, $h\nu = 3.3 \cdot 10^{-21}$ J.

$$\therefore T = \frac{3.3 \cdot 10^{-21}}{1.38 \cdot 10^{-23}} \text{ K}$$

$$\approx 240 \text{ K}$$

Remember that ν is dependent on the mass of the atom, so the Einstein temperature varies from one substance to another. This temperature is generally significantly below room temperature, which is why the restriction on energies of a vibrating system remained undiscovered until this century.

Let us look now at the question of deciding how many atoms will be in each of the permitted energy states. We can do this by utilizing the results of an Exercise along similar lines in Unit 4.

SAQ 16 (Revision)   If the gap between permitted energy levels is $h\nu$, write down an expression showing how the number of atoms having the nth energy level varies with temperature.

ANSWER $N_n = A\mathrm{e}^{-nh\nu/kT}$ (A is a constant)

If you are unsure of the Boltzmann factor, it would do no harm to revise it (Unit 4, Section 4.4.1). Using this relation and the fact that we are always considering large numbers of atoms, it is possible to derive an expression for the average energy of a vibrating atom restricted to discrete energy levels. The total energy of N such atoms is given by:

$$U = \frac{Nh\nu}{\mathrm{e}^{h\nu/kT} - 1}$$

When T is large compared with $h\nu/k$, the expression reduces to NkT. I hope that you would expect this from your knowledge that each atom has (on average) a total energy of kT for each vibration. We shall now, in Section 8.2.5, examine the application of the exact result at low temperatures to explain some peculiar measurements of heat capacity.

8.2.5   Heat capacity at low temperatures

You may well be wondering why we have gone to so much trouble to describe the limitations on energy levels when an oscillating atom is at a low temperature. Einstein developed this whole theory to account for some strange experimental results when heat capacities were measured at low temperatures. As an example, we shall consider copper. Its molar heat capacity at room temperature is 24.6 $J \, mol^{-1} \, K^{-1}$.

SAQ 17 (Revision)   Is this a typical value for the molar heat capacity of a material?

ANSWER   It certainly is—you should recall that a whole range of materials have molar heat capacities about 25 $J \, mol^{-1} \, K^{-1}$, and that this is in accordance with the prediction of our model that the molar heat capacity will be 3 $N_A k$ $J \, mol^{-1} \, K^{-1}$.

When the molar heat capacity of copper was measured at low temperatures, the values obtained were significantly smaller: 22.2 at 173 K, 11.6 at 73 K and 0.86 at 23 K. In fact, the heat capacity tends to zero at the absolute zero of temperature. Our simple model of a mechanical oscillator has no behaviour that provides an analogue to this effect.

Einstein suggested that the possible energy levels of an atomic oscillator might be restricted to certain discrete values, and showed that if this were true the average energy for each of a number of oscillators would be given by:

$$U = \frac{h\nu}{e^{h\nu/kT} - 1}$$

This expression reduced to kT for large values of T (i.e. room temperature and above), so it is in accord with the classical result. At lower temperatures, its value decreases—you can probably see at a glance that the denominator becomes large as T is reduced. If you have sufficient time, it is instructive to compute the average energy for a few temperatures, assuming $\nu \approx 5.10^{12} \, s^{-1}$. The results of such a computation are in quite good agreement with experiment, as shown in Figure 10.

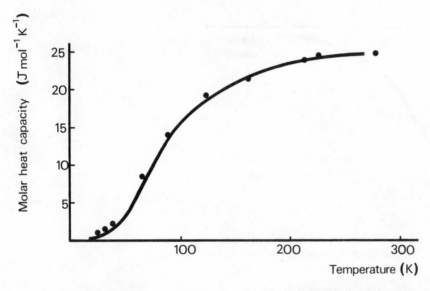

Figure 10   Einstein model for the molar heat capacity of copper.

The Einstein model is by no means perfect, and this is hardly surprising. It assumes, for example, that the atoms in a solid vibrate independently. Why might this be a source of error?

You should remember (from Section 8.2.3 and Home Experiment 8.3) that linked oscillators interact, transferring energy from one to another. More complex models, such as the Debye model, have been proposed to account for the behaviour of heat capacity at low temperatures. If you are interested in pursuing this subject further, it is discussed in some detail in Tabor, *Gases, Liquids and Solids**, Section 10.1.3 and more briefly in Flowers and Mendoza, *Properties of Matter***, section 9.5.2.

* D. Tabor (1969) *Gases, liquids and solids*, Penguin Books.

** B. H. Flowers and E. Mendoza (1970) *Properties of Matter*, John Wiley.

8.2.6 Summary

It is possible to measure the heat capacity of an object experimentally, either by measuring the temperature rise caused by supplying a known amount of heat, or by comparison with a substance of known heat capacity in the method of mixtures.

For a whole range of materials, the molar heat capacity is observed to be about 25 J mol^{-1} K^{-1}. This relation is known as the Dulong-Petit law.

The force curve for interaction between atoms suggests that an atom displaced from equilibrium will experience a restoring force.

Comparison with a mechanical analogue suggests that the kinetic energy which an atom possesses, by virtue of the temperature, could give rise to a vibration about the equilibrium position.

By analogy with the mechanical model, it is possible to estimate the atomic vibration frequency as about 10^{13} s^{-1}. The model also suggests that the frequency depends on the mass of the atom.

These considerations enable us to revise the potential-energy curve to take account of the kinetic energy, and the graph then indicates the approximate amplitude of the atomic vibration (Fig. 11).

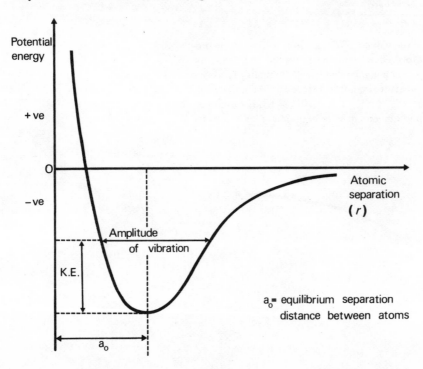

Figure 11   Energy curve for atoms in a solid.

Using the relation between temperature and mean kinetic energy of atoms, it can be shown that the total energy of each atom at temperature T is (on average) $3 kT$.

The total energy of a mole of any atomic solid is therefore $3 N_A kT$, and hence the molar heat capacity is $3 N_A k$ J mol^{-1} K^{-1}. This result is in very good agreement with the Dulong-Petit law.

Even at room temperature, the amplitude of atomic vibrations is a significant fraction of the interatomic separation.

The vibrating atom interacts with its neighbours, and energy may be transferred as a result.

A sudden pulse of energy applied to one end of a solid leads to energy transfer through the solid. The velocity of this elastic wave in the solid may be computed from the atomic vibration frequency, and the result is in good agreement with experiment.

Atoms vibrating in a solid may only have certain specific values of energy. This restriction is unimportant at room temperature, but becomes very significant at low temperatures.

18

The Einstein model of heat capacity is based on this restriction of allowed energies, and affords an explanation for the dramatically reduced values of heat capacity at low temperatures.

8.3 Thermal expansion of solids

This Section examines another thermal property of solids—their expansion when heated. We start by looking at the useful and annoying manifestations of this property, and develop analytical expressions to predict the amount by which a given solid will expand. Our model of the solid is examined in the light of this experimental evidence. Melting of solids is also briefly discussed in the light of the model.

8.3.1 General description of expansion

It is almost common knowledge that solids expand when heated. The housewife who loosens a stubborn screwtop lid from a glass jar with hot water is taking practical advantage of the effect. It is very important to allow for expansion in large constructions. Small gaps were usually left between sections of railway line, until the comparatively recent development of ingenious sliding joints. Pipes carrying steam have loops to allow for expansion, and bridges compensate for changes in length by means of a hinge or a roller. For any given material, the length of an object will increase quite predictably with temperature. The expansion at normal temperatures is linearly dependent on the rise in temperature, so that if a length l_0 is heated through T Kelvin it will expand to a length l_T, given by:

$$l_T = l_0 (1 + \alpha T)$$

The constant α is called the coefficient of linear expansion for the material. For most metals, the value of α is of the order of 10^{-5} K^{-1}. This means that a metal rod heated by 100 K increases its length by about 0·1 per cent, which is small but certainly measurable.

SAQ 18   A bridge span has a length of 300 metres at 0 °C. Given that α for steel is $1.1 \cdot 10^{-5}$ per kelvin, determine the increase in the length of the bridge on a hot day when the temperature is 30 °C.

ANSWER   The length at 30 °C is given by $l_{30} = l_0 (1 + 30\alpha)$

$$= 300 (1 + 3.3 \times 10^{-4}) \, \text{m}$$

The *increase* in length is clearly $l_{30} - l_0$

$$= 300 \times 3.3 \times 10^{-4} \, \text{m}$$

$$\approx 0.1 \, \text{m}$$

Obviously increases in length cause surface areas to expand. Consider the simple case of a square which has sides initially of length l_0, and call its initial area A_0, clearly $A_0 = l_0^2$. If the material is now heated through T kelvin, it will expand and the area will increase.

SAQ 19   Obtain an expression for the new area, A_T, in terms of A_0, T and the coefficient of linear expansion, α.

ANSWER
$$A_T = l_T^2$$
$$= [l_0 (1 + \alpha T)]^2$$
$$= l_0^2 (1 + \alpha T)^2$$
$$= A_0 (1 + \alpha T)^2$$
$$= A_0 (1 + 2\alpha T + (\alpha T)^2)$$

In most cases, αT is small, and so $(\alpha T)^2$ is very small indeed. If αT is 1 per cent, for instance, $(\alpha T)^2$ is one part in ten thousand. We can neglect this term and express the expanded area as $A_T = A_0 (1 + 2\alpha T)$.

19

Can you see how the volume of a solid object will increase with temperature? A similar argument gives $V_T = V_0 (1 + 3\alpha T)$.

8.3.2 Uses of thermal expansion

Thermal expansion is a property of materials often put to practical use. It is easy to see how a cut-out switch could be made by arranging that a strip of metal expanded to close an electrical circuit at some predetermined temperature. In practice, for any ordinary change in temperature, the amount by which a short strip of metal expands is small. Most simple devices for control of temperature, such as oven thermostats in domestic cookers, use a more subtle application of this effect. Strips of two different metals are fixed together so that they form a straight bimetallic strip. If the strip is heated, usually one metal will expand more than the other, and so the strip will bend into a curve. Designing a practical device naturally involves choosing two metals having significantly different expansion coefficients. A popular choice is zinc ($\alpha = 3.5 \cdot 10^{-5}$ per K) with iron ($\alpha = 1.1 \cdot 10^{-5}$ per K), as these have respectively the highest and lowest values of α among metals in common use. The amount of bending in a bimetallic strip depends on the difference between the two expansion coefficients, the rise in temperature and the thickness of the strip. A mathematical expression for the curvature of the strip in terms of these factors can be calculated, but it is probably more useful for our purposes to consider a practical example. A straight bimetallic strip made from zinc and iron, having a total thickness of 2 mm and a length of 10 cm, would bend at a typical oven temperature (350 °F) so that its radius of curvature would be 25 cm. In other words, if one end of the strip is fixed, the other end will have bent about 1 cm from the straight line. In a typical thermostat for a domestic oven, bending caused by a temperature above the setting closes an electrical contact and cuts off the power. When the oven temperature falls, the curvature of the strip decreases and the power is applied again. You can observe this effect for yourself by doing Home Experiment 8.4. It would be appropriate to do it at this point—only 5–10 minutes should be needed.

8.3.3 Why does a solid expand?

There is ample evidence that solids do expand when heated. Examples range from your Home Experiment to the occasional buckling of railway lines in hot climates. This observation poses an obvious question: why do solids behave in this way? The purpose of this Section of the Unit is to show how this behaviour of real solids affects our simple model.

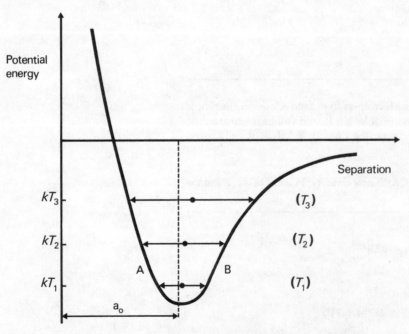

Figure 12 Energy-distance curve, showing thermal expansion.

By now you should be quite familiar with the way an atom's potential energy depends on the distance from its neighbour. The curve shown in Figure 12 is basically the same as the one used several times in earlier parts of this Course.

In this diagram, a_0 is the mean separation at very low temperatures. As the temperature increases, so does the average energy per atom, which you remember as being $\frac{1}{2}kT$ for each degree of freedom. The three lines on the curve represent the amplitudes of an atom's vibrations at successively higher temperatures T_1, T_2, T_3. As the energy of an atom increases, so it becomes free to vibrate over a larger distance, just as a child on a swing will go further from the central position if a more strenuous push is applied. Thus the amplitude of vibration at T_3 is greater than at lower temperatures. A wider range of vibration does not, however, explain expansion—the *central position* of the child on his swing remains the same, irrespective of the vigour of his swinging. The experimental observation that solids expand when heated must be reflected in our model if it is to remain plausible. Accordingly, we need to modify the model to account for the conclusions drawn from experiment.

The motion of a swing, or a pendulum, is symmetric because the force returning the object to its equilibrium position—the gravitational attraction of the Earth—is the same on both sides. This is a characteristic of the harmonic oscillator, which we have found such a useful analogy to the vibrating atoms in a solid. Now we find it necessary to vary the model slightly. Since the average distance between atoms increases with temperature, it must be easier for an atom to move away from its neighbour than to move close to it. The force opposing an atom as it moves towards its neighbour, then, must be greater than the force acting on it as it moves away. The motion is thus not symmetric, and the oscillator is *anharmonic*. If you lóok back to Figure 12, you will see that the energy curve we have been using already incorporates this feature. The curve slopes more steeply in region A than in region B, so as an atom moves to a position of higher energy it finds it easier to move away from its neighbour than to move towards it. This means that the mid-point of the atom's vibration becomes further away from its neighbour as the temperature rises. The dots on the graph show the mean separation distances at successively higher temperatures T_1, T_2 and T_3. At the atomic level, the size of this increase is not large in absolute terms. When, however, every atom in a solid moves slightly further from each neighbour, the overall increase in the dimensions of the solid is quite noticeable.

The simple model which has been so useful for explaining the thermal behaviour of solids must be slightly modified in the light of knowledge of thermal expansion. It seems that atoms vibrate as *anharmonic oscillators*, rather than following the laws of S.H.M. Remember that coefficients of thermal expansion are quite small, of the order of 10^{-5} K^{-1}, so the degree of departure from S.H.M. is sufficiently small for our earlier results to remain valid approximations. The model needs relatively minor modification.

anharmonic oscillator

In Section 8.2, we analysed the specific heat of a solid by considering each atom as a vibrating particle. The same approach has now been developed to obtain a physical picture of the mechanism responsible for thermal expansion. In 1908, Grüneisen analysed published values of α, the coefficient of linear expansion, and c_V, the specific heat capacity* at constant volume, for various metals. He reached the conclusion that they are related: α/c_V is an approximately constant ratio, almost the same value for any metals.

SAQ 20   Can you suggest why these properties of a substance should appear to be linked?

ANSWER   Both specific heat arid thermal expansion arise from atomic vibrations, so it is not surprising that they are roughly related. The model required quite minor modification to account for expansion.

The relation can be taken further. It is possible to develop a mathematical formalism for thermal expansion, the most usual approach being to approximate the anharmonic curve by an algebraic expression (see Tabor, section 10.2).

---

* This Unit has been cast mainly in terms of molar heat capacities, but it is also quite common to talk of a substance's *specific heat capacity*—the heat capacity per unit mass, measured in J kg^{-1} K^{-1}.

Both α and c_V can then be expressed in terms of the coefficients of a power series. This treatment leads to analytical proof of the link between the two parameters. The relationship is known as *Grüneisen's law*. Like some other results we have developed from the mechanical model of atoms in a solid, it is valid provided you are not squeamish about factors of two!

This table lists values of α and c_V for seven metals. As an exercise, calculate the missing values of the ratio c_V/α and observe with wonder the strengths and deficiencies of Grüneisen's law.

Substance	Specific heat capacity /kg^{-1} K^{-1}	Expansion coefficient /10^{-6} K^{-1}	$C_V/\alpha \times 10^6$
Tin	226	23	9.9
Magnesium	246	25	9.9
Gold	132	14	
Zinc	385	31	
Silver	235	19	
Platinum	136	9	
Copper	385	17	

9.5, 12.4, 12.4, 15.1, 22.6. Note that the answers are all within a factor of two (roughly!), so the link between the properties is credible.

8.3.4 Melting

We all know that a solid does not just expand if its temperature is increased: eventually a temperature will be reached at which the solid melts. Melting is a considerable embarrassment to our simple picture of solids built up from the potential energy curve. This curve alone really only explains the solid state, in which the atoms do not have sufficient energy to escape from their neighbours, and the gaseous state, in which atoms charge freely around. As the structure and properties of the liquid state are to be discussed in Units 9 and 10, I will not say any more about the subject here. We can, however, obtain a very simple-minded law for melting from our model.

Consider the table below, listing the melting points of a range of metals with their coefficients of thermal expansion. What do you notice?

Material	M.P./K	$\alpha/10^{-6}$ K^{-1}
Mercury	234	40
Lead	600	29
Aluminium	933	25
Copper	1 356	17
Iron	1 812	12
Tungsten	3 653	4.2

You may have noticed that there is a general tendency for metals with high melting points to have low coefficients of thermal expansion, and vice versa. We could explain the correlation observed here by suggesting that melting point is related to the depth of the trough in the potential energy curve. Remember that thermal expansion is due to asymmetry of this trough, so it would not be unreasonable to argue that a deeper one would have a more symmetrical shape at the bottom. This idea is illustrated in Figure 13, which shows the potential energy curves for three materials having quite different troughs. If the inter-atomic distances are broadly the same, so that the curves tend to zero at roughly the same spacing, clearly the deeper troughs will be more symmetric. Hence, if substances having deep energy troughs have high melting points, they can also be expected to exhibit low values of thermal expansion.

Although that argument is plausible, it is only qualitative. A better picture of melting can be obtained from our knowledge of atomic vibrations.

22

SAQ 21 (Revision)   What is the amplitude of the atomic vibrations in a solid at temperature T?

ANSWER   The amplitude of vibrations at temperature T is given by

$$A = \sqrt{\frac{2\,k\,T}{f}} \qquad \text{where } f \text{ is the force constant.}$$

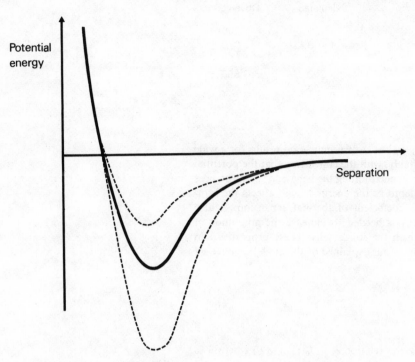

Potential energy

Separation

Figure 13   Variation of symmetry with trough depth.

It is possible to use this result and our earlier expression of the force constant, f, in terms of known parameters to obtain a rough model for melting. You should recall that f is equal to the product of the Young modulus of the particular material, E, and its average interatomic distance, a_0, i.e. $f = a_0\,E$.

Hence:

$$A = \sqrt{\frac{2\,k\,T}{a_0\,E}}$$

This expression relates the amplitude of an atom's vibrations to temperature, and we are reminded that increasing the temperature causes each atom to oscillate over a greater distance. Knowing that the structure of a solid 'loosens-up' as it melts, Lindemann proposed that the melting point of an atomic solid could be estimated from the energy curve by assuming that melting occurs when the vibration amplitude exceeds some critical fraction of the interatomic spacing —the same fraction for all solids. This is Lindemann's law of melting. He argued that energy transfer between neighbours would increase rapidly beyond this critical amplitude, and so the crystal structure would disintegrate.

Lindemann's law of melting

Taking our expression for the vibration amplitude, let us assume that it is some fraction β of the interatomic spacing a_0 at the melting point, i.e. when $T = T_m$.

$$\text{Then } A = \beta a_0 = \sqrt{\frac{2\,k\,T_m}{a_0\,E}}$$

Removing the square root by squaring both sides of the equation

$$\beta^2 a_0^2 = \frac{2\,k\,T_m}{a_0\,E}$$

which can be rearranged to give:

$$T_m = \frac{\beta^2\,a_0^3\,E}{2k}$$

Now we have an expression for the melting point in terms of the interatomic spacing a_0, the Young modulus E and the Boltzmann constant k, together with the fraction β. Lindemann tried various values of β, matching calculations with experiment, and came to the conclusion that melting occurs when the amplitude of atomic vibrations exceeded one-seventh of the interatomic spacing. The table gives some calculations based on this value, taking $\beta^2 \approx 1/50$.

Material	Melting point/K	
	Calculated	Observed
Lead	400	600
Silver	1 100	1 270
Iron	1 800	1 800
Tungsten	4 200	3 650
Quartz	1 900	2 000
Sodium chloride	1 200	1 070

Considering how crude the model is, it gives surprisingly good results for a wide range of materials. We are left, inevitably, with the conclusion that the potential energy curve is again a critical factor in determining the behaviour of substances when heat energy is supplied. The depth of the energy trough affects the symmetry at its bottom, and hence the coefficient of thermal expansion. It also determines how much thermal energy is needed to increase the amplitude of atomic vibrations to the level at which the solid melts. These properties join specific heat on our list of areas of behaviour explained by the model we have set up in this Unit.

8.3.5 Summary

Solids expand when heated, obeying the relation $l_T = l_0 (1 + \alpha T)$ where α is the coefficient of thermal expansion.

The difference between expansion coefficients for different materials is exploited in devices such as the bimetallic strip.

Thermal expansion implies that the trough of the potential energy curve is not symmetric. This conclusion leads to a modification of our mechanical model to take account of this anharmonic oscillation.

Analysis of data shows an approximate link between α and c_V for a range of materials. This relationship is known as Grüneisen's law.

An approximate model of melting is obtained by assuming that a solid will melt when the amplitude of atomic vibrations exceeds some critical fraction of the interatomic distance. This is Lindemann's law, and gives fair agreement with experiment.

Thermal expansion and melting are both explained quite well by a model of the atom as an anharmonic oscillator.

8.4   Thermal conductivity

8.4.1   General principles

The laws of heat flow in solids arise from two principles, both of which are little more than common sense. The rate at which heat flows through a solid increases if the temperature difference across it becomes larger: even a mere male in the kitchen knows that the water in a saucepan boils more rapidly if the temperature of the heating element is turned up! Secondly, the rate of heat flow through a solid is proportional to its cross-sectional area: all other things being equal (including power per unit area) a given volume of water will boil more quickly in a larger saucepan of the same thickness. Combining these principles, the rate of heat flow through a solid (dQ/dt) is proportional to the temperature gradient (dT/dx) and the cross-sectional area (dA). The proportionality can be made an equation by introducing a constant, K, defined as the thermal conductivity of the material:

$$\frac{dQ}{dt} = - K\,dA\,\frac{dT}{dx}$$

What is the significance of the minus?

8.4.2 Thermal diffusivity

The most common problem in heat flow is the situation in which heat is supplied to one surface of a body and we want to know how the temperature somewhere else varies with time. Using our culinary example again, if heat is supplied to the base of a saucepan, we might want to know how quickly the temperature rises at the inside surface. When heat energy is supplied to one end of a body clearly it will heat up and therefore absorb some of the heat.

Take a small volume element of the solid, dx long, with a cross-sectional area dA (Fig. 14). Let the temperature at one side be T, and that at the other $T + dT$. We may now analyse the heat flow in terms of our equation.

$$\text{Heat flow into elementary volume} = - K\,dA\,\frac{dT}{dx}$$

$$\text{Heat flow out of elementary volume} = - K\,dA\,\frac{d}{dx}(T + dT)$$

The rate at which heat accumulates in the volume element is given by $K\,dA\,\partial^2 T/\partial x^2\,dx$. The temperature rise this causes will be determined by the heat capacity of the element, which we will calculate in terms of its mass and the specific heat capacity of the material. The mass will be given by the product of the volume ($dA\,dx$) and the density of the material ρ. If the specific heat capacity is c, the rate of temperature rise $\partial T/\partial t$ will be given by

$$(c\rho\,dA\,dx)\frac{\partial T}{\partial t} = K\,dA\,\frac{\partial^2 T}{\partial x^2}\,dx$$

Simplifying

$$\frac{\partial T}{\partial t} = \frac{K}{\rho c} \cdot \frac{\partial^2 T}{\partial x^2}$$

The quantity $K/\rho c$, which will be a constant for any given material, is usually called the *thermal diffusivity*. Can you guess why?

The equation is identical in form to the one-dimensional diffusion equation,

$$\frac{\partial c}{\partial t} = D\,\frac{\partial^2 c}{\partial x^2}$$

which gives the change in the concentration of particles with time ($\partial c/\partial t$) as a function of their spatial distribution and a diffusion coefficient D. This mathematical similarity suggests a physical picture for heat flow, implying that heat diffuses through a solid like a molecule moving about in a gas. This behaviour of thermal energy, almost as if it were being carried by particles, leads to a theory for heat flow in solids. The theory is the subject of the next Section.

8.4.3 Theory of thermal conductivity

A simple theory for thermal conductivity is based on the parallel we have just drawn with diffusion, explaining the transfer of heat by a collision process which transfers thermal energy from hot parts of a solid to the colder regions. In a gas, where heat is transferred by collisions, the thermal conductivity can be shown to be given by

$$K = \tfrac{1}{3}n \times \bar{v} \times \lambda\,c_V$$

where $\bar{v}$ is the average velocity of molecules, n the number of molecules per unit volume and λ the mean free path between collisions*. Since c_V in this equation

* See Tabor, section 4.5.2, if you are interested in the derivation of this expression.

Since heat flows from a hotter point to a cooler one, a positive flow of heat corresponds to a negative temperature gradient.

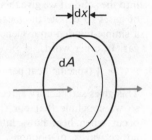

Figure 14

thermal diffusivity

is the specific heat per molecule, we may combine it with n to give the specific heat per unit volume:

$$K = \tfrac{1}{3} (nc_v) \, \bar{v} \, \lambda$$

We know from earlier Sections of this Unit that thermal energy is carried through a crystal by means of lattice vibrations. If heat is applied to one end of a solid, the atoms at that end will have more energy (on average) and so will vibrate with greater amplitudes. The energy will be transmitted to the neighbouring atoms and on into the solid as a lattice vibration, or *phonon*. Generated at the hot end, the vibrations move into the solid with the velocity of a sound wave until eventually all their energy is distributed into the lattice. All this is exactly in line with the approach we developed in Section 8.2.3. Now it seems reasonable to suggest that the rate of heat flow into the solid depends on the average distance a phonon travels before its energy is redistributed to the solid—clearly the further into the lattice each phonon carries its energy, the more rapidly heat is transported into the solid. If we give this average distance the symbol λ, used in the treatment of gases to denote the mean free path between collisions, we have established a simple-minded equivalence with the expression for thermal conductivity in a gas. In other words,

$$K = \tfrac{1}{3} \text{ (specific heat per unit volume)} \times \text{(velocity of sound waves)} \times \lambda$$

This gives satisfactory agreement with measurements for most poor conductors, so we conclude that our simple model explains the physical processes which occur when heat flows into a solid. Thermal energy is transmitted through lattice waves, or phonons, travelling into the solid with the velocity of sound and dissipating their energy into the lattice after travelling an average distance λ. Generally λ is about 20 Å (or 2.10^{-9} m), so an average phonon travels through about ten interatomic distances before its energy is distributed in the crystal lattice.

Most metals are good thermal conductors, typically having values of K more than 100 times greater than for insulating solids. This suggests that a different mechanism is responsible for carrying heat through metals. Since metals are also generally good conductors of electricity, it would not be illogical to suspect that the two properties are related. So they are, but the reasons are beyond the scope of this Course*

Home Experiment 8.5 illustrates the variation in thermal conductivity between materials. You should do the experiment at this point.

8.4.4 Summary

The rate of heat flow through a solid is proportional both to its cross-sectional area and the temperature difference across it.

A mathematical similarity suggests that heat is carried into a solid by a diffusion-like process.

Rate of heat flow into a solid depends on the average distance a phonon travels before its energy is distributed into the lattice. Phonons travel at the speed of sound, and generally travel about ten interatomic distances before all their energy is distributed.

8.5 Point defects

Crystals do not usually have a perfectly ordered lattice structure of the type described in Unit 7. Almost invariably there will be various defects present. This subject of defects is a complex one, so I will look only at localized faults in crystals. These are generally known as *point defects*. The most common types of point defects are missing atoms, atoms displaced from their normal sites, and foreign atoms substituted in the lattice. The number of most types of defects in

---

* There is a brief discussion of the relationship in Tabor, section 10.4, and a rather fuller treatment in Flowers and Mendoza, section 8.6.

a crystal depends very sensitively on temperature, so the formation and movement of defects form an important section of thermal properties. Several types of defects will be described in this Section, and then we will discuss the effect of temperature on the number of defects. Section 8.6 will go on to the movement of defects, which is the basis of *diffusion* in solids.

diffusion

8.5.1 Vacancies, interstitials and impurity atoms

The simplest possible type of defect is the *vacancy*, which is simply a missing atom—a hole in the crystal where an atom would normally be found (Fig. 15)

vacancy

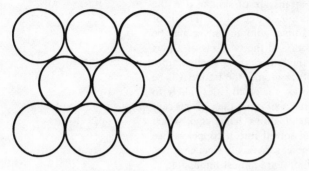

Figure 15   A vacancy in a close-packed plane of atoms.

Vacancies are likely to be present in any crystal, as a consequence of fluctuations in thermal energy. Quite large concentrations of vacancies may be produced if a crystal lattice is brutally deformed, e.g. by hammering or cold rolling. Normally, at room temperature, only about one atomic site in 10^{12} will be vacant in a metal.

SAQ 22   How many lattice sites will be vacant in a mole of aluminium at room temperature?

ANSWER   About 10^{11} sites will be vacant, in a volume of about 10 cubic centimetres (10^{-5} m^3).

An *interstitial* atom is the opposite of the vacancy—an extra atom squeezed into the crystal lattice, fitting between atoms occupying normal sites (Fig. 16).

interstitial

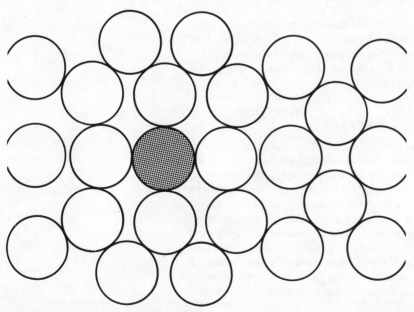

Figure 16   An interstitial in a plane of atoms.

Obviously this is not very likely to happen in a close-packed structure, like the metal crystals you have examined in Unit 7. It does happen, however, in some looser structures, such as germanium and the silver halides. A second type of interstitial defect is also the first of another group—*impurity defects*. Even

impurity defects

close-packed structures contain small tetrahedral and octahedral gaps between atoms, and these gaps may be large enough to accommodate smaller atoms. For example, carbon atoms fit into interstitial sites between iron atoms—an effect at atomic level which plays an important role in the use of iron and steel. Hydrogen atoms flit into and out of interstitial sites in metal lattices so easily that a basic limitation on the performance of steel ultra-high-vacuum systems is the need to pump out hydrogen leaking in from the atmosphere! Small foreign atoms can occupy significant numbers of interstitial sites in even a close-packed lattice.

Another type of impurity defect is the real cuckoo in the nest—a foreign atom occupying a regular lattice site (Fig. 17). If the atoms are of similar size, the substitution may be effected with very little distortion of the lattice. This is of great importance in the mixing of metals; for example, gold and silver may be mixed in any proportions to form a solid solution, and the two sets of atoms are mixed randomly among the possible sites on the lattice. If the foreign atom is of markedly different size from the regular lattice atoms, the lattice will be distorted. Since distorting the lattice requires energy, the atom is less likely to find a happy home. As a general rule, a size difference of more than 15 per cent is thought to be unfavourable for the formation of alloys. Thus zinc, which adjoins copper on the Periodic Table, may be dissolved into a copper lattice until it occupies nearly 40 per cent of the sites, whereas markedly smaller atoms (e.g. lithium) and markedly larger ones (e.g. thallium) are almost impossible to introduce into the lattice.

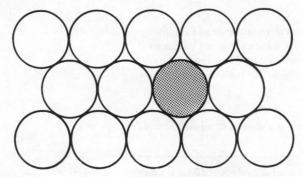

Figure 17   Impurity in a close-packed plane.

To summarize, the most important types of point defects are vacancies, impurities and interstitials. All may well be present in some quantity in a solid, but generally one type of defect will predominate—the type which requires least energy for formation.

Finally, you should appreciate that compounds in solid form lead to more complicated defects. This is particularly the case for ionic solids, as they are composed of ions, which means that vacancies have an effective electrical charge. A whole zoo of complex defects result, some of them not yet fully understood, so we will not venture into that territory in this Course.

8.5.2   Temperature-dependence of defect density

Producing a defect in an otherwise perfect crystal lattice requires energy. As a simple instance, you could say that the energy required to produce a vacancy is the energy needed to take an atom from the body of the crystal and place it on the surface. Obviously that is an oversimplified picture—atoms do not leap dramatically from the deep interior of a crystal to the surface. It is observed, however, that the number of defects in a lattice is very strongly dependent on temperature. If the energy needed to create a vacancy is assumed to have a fixed value, E_v, we can use the Boltzmann function again to work out the temperature-dependence. Since the relative probability of an atom in a solid at temperature T having an energy E is $e^{-E_v/kT}$, the probability of any chosen atomic site being vacant will also have that value. If the crystal contains N atomic sites, the number vacant at temperature T will be given by

$$n_v = N e^{-E_v/kT}$$

Experimental determinations of defect densities bear out this rule. A characteristic energy is needed to create a defect in a given material, and the value of the energy may be calculated by determining n_v experimentally and plotting log n_v against $1/T$, giving E_v/k as the slope of the graph. The exponential increase with temperature means that crystals rapidly become less ordered as the temperature is raised.

Whereas only 1 atomic site in 10^{12} is vacant in aluminium at room temperature, near the melting point the proportion is about 1 in 1000—a ratio typical of metals just below their melting points. Just as vacancy concentrations increase exponentially with temperature, so do the concentrations of other defects.

SAQ 23   What determines which defect will be most prevalent in any given solid?

ANSWER   The energies of formation for the various defects—the most prevalent defect in the solid will be that which requires least energy for its formation.

SAQ 24   List the most important types of point defects in solids.

ANSWER   Vacancies; interstitial atoms; impurity atoms.

SAQ 25   How does the number of vacancies in a given lattice vary with temperature?

ANSWER   The number of vacancies, n_v, at a temperature T is given by

$$n_v = N e^{-E_v/kT}$$

where E_v is the characteristic energy for production of a vacancy in that lattice.

8.6   Transport processes

I have discussed some of the point defects which occur in solids, and suggested that the density of such defects depends on the thermal energy of the lattice. We will now examine some of the implications of defects in a crystal lattice. Think of a lattice plane containing a vacant site (Fig. 18). If one of the atoms

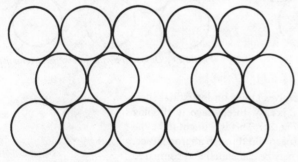

Figure 18   Lattice plane containing a vacancy.

adjacent to the vacancy were to undergo an extremely energetic vibration, might it not leave its site completely and move into the vacant site? Atoms wandering around the lattice by such a process would be undergoing diffusion, just as molecules in a gas do. In fact, diffusion does occur in solids, although usually quite slowly at room temperature. The process becomes much more rapid at higher temperatures, so we will examine diffusion as a temperature-dependent property. In the first instance, we will discuss how individual atoms can move about; then the overall effects on the solid will be considered. Diffusion in solids has several important applications in technology, so a brief summary of these completes the Unit text.

8.6.1   Mechanisms for movement of atoms

When explanations were being sought for the observation that diffusion does take place in solids, the first theory was that adjacent atoms simply exchange places. With your knowledge of the close-packed structure of many metals, you should find such an explanation difficult to swallow—consider the distortion of the lattice necessary for the two adjacent atoms in Figure 19 to change places. Ingenious attempts to salvage the theory by suggesting that three or four atoms rotate as a group have been made, but there is no evidence of such an unlikely degree of cooperation among atoms. It is a much more plausible suggestion

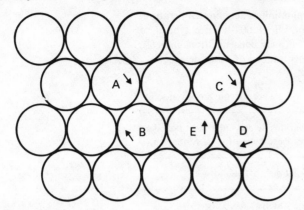

Figure 19   Distortions of a lattice plane to allow exchanges.

that diffusion occurs by means of atoms jumping into vacant lattice sites, as shown in Figure 20. Knowing what we do about energies of atoms, it is possible to make calculations of the energy needed for an atom to make such a jump. These calculations can be compared with experimental results, as we will discuss in Section 8.6.2. It is generally accepted that diffusion occurs by this process in face-centred-cubic metals and alloys, as well as some metals with other crystal structures. Diffusion by jumping to vacant lattice sites also happens in ionic solids (e.g. NaCl) and some metallic oxides.

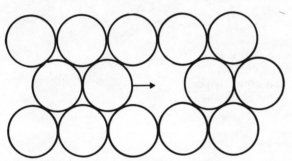

Figure 20   Diffusion by the vacancy mechanism.

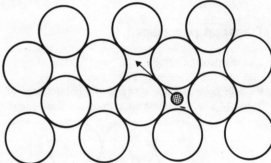

Figure 21   Diffusion by the interstitial mechanism.

The other principal mechanism for diffusion involves atoms on interstitial sites. If a small atom occupies an interstitial site, it is easy to envisage it slipping between the lattice atoms to another such site (Fig. 21). This is thought to be the mechanism by which atoms of carbon and hydrogen slip through an iron lattice. Again, the energy needed to make such a jump may be calculated and compared with experiment.

There are more complicated mechanisms of diffusion thought to apply in some systems, but we shall restrict our discussion to the two cases just mentioned: atoms jumping to a vacant lattice site, and atoms slipping through a lattice from one interstitial site to the next.

8.6.2   How far will an atom travel?

The next problem is to work out how quickly we would expect an atom to diffuse into a solid, given that we know the mechanism by which it moves. Suppose we could label one atom in the middle of a solid (with a dab of red paint?) and watch its progress—how would it move? If it was diffusing by jumping to adjoining vacant lattice sites, its progress would be a sequence of such jumps with no systematic direction—each jump could be towards *any* of the nearest-neighbour sites. It performs what is known as a *random walk*. The fact that the movement is random means that the problem can be attacked statistically. Home Experiment 8.6 is a simple introduction to random walk, so it would be appropriate to do the experiment at this stage.

random walk

With any luck, you will have discovered from your experiment that it is impossible to predict the direction an atom will take in its random walk. You may be able to estimate how far from the origin an atom is likely, on average, to be after a given number of jumps, but it is unlikely that your simple experiment will have given you enough information.

There are two possible ways of making a good estimate. You could 'follow' an atom over an enormous number of jumps in a simulation experiment*, or you could attempt a mathematical analysis of the problem. Both these approaches lead to the conclusion that the root-mean-square displacement of a particle after a random walk is proportional to the square root of the number of jumps. In other words, if several atoms make n jumps of length d, the r.m.s. distance travelled will be approximately $d\sqrt{n}$. This is a very significant result, as it leads directly to an estimate of diffusion rates in solids.

SAQ 26   Why do you think we have taken the r.m.s. displacement rather than the mean?

ANSWER   Since the particles are just as likely to jump in any arbitrarily-defined positive direction as in the corresponding negative direction, the mean displacement will be zero. Squaring gives the mean magnitude of all displacements, regardless of direction.

Recalling our picture of diffusion by the vacancy mechanism in a close-packed lattice, we could say that the distance of an atom's jump is approximately one atomic diameter. That means that an atom will (on average) have moved $\sqrt{n}$ atomic diameters after n jumps, and since the atomic diameter can be given a reasonably accurate value, measuring the average distance travelled leads to a good estimate of the number of jumps made. Knowing how many jumps have been made in a given time would tell us how often an atom jumps to an adjacent lattice site. Considering an atom adjacent to a vacancy, there are two things which determine whether the atom will jump. It must be travelling towards the vacancy, and it must have sufficient energy to squeeze past other atoms into the vacant site. Since the atom is vibrating, it will be travelling towards the vacancy once in every complete oscillation—the diffusion rate should be proportional to the frequency of vibration. Since it also requires a given amount of energy to make a jump, we know the probability of the atom having that energy will vary according to a Boltzmann-type factor. In line with practice in other areas, we will call this critical energy the *activation energy for diffusion*, Q. Then the jump rate should be proportional to ν and to the probability that an atom at temperature T will have this energy, $e^{-Q/kT}$. Thus determining how far, on average, an atom travels in a given time leads to an estimate of the number of jumps made, and repeating the experiment for different temperatures should (according to our model) allow the energy needed for diffusion to be calculated. The only hitch is—how do you find out how far an atom has moved? Our approach has been based on choosing an atom and watching it move, but atoms are indistinguishable—what can we do to make them identifiable?

activation energy for diffusion

This problem was seemingly insuperable until about 1950, when the ready availability of radioactive isotopes provided an elegant solution. Suppose a layer of radioactive atoms is placed (by evaporation or electro-plating) on the surface of our solid. The atoms will gradually perform random-walk motions into the solid. If we later slice up the solid and measure the radioactivity in each slice, a profile of the relative numbers of atoms in the different slices can be built up. It is thus possible to estimate how far, on average, each atom has travelled. Repeating the experiment over a range of temperatures allows the activation energy for diffusion to be calculated. This method of determining diffusion rates by following radioactive tracers has been of great significance in determining the way atoms move in solids.

In general, atoms diffuse very slowly in solids at room temperature. As you would expect, the diffusion rate increases exponentially with rising temperature. The chromium plating on a car bumper does not diffuse into the steel beneath

* This is done by computer simulation in the TV programme associated with this Unit.

to any noticeable extent at normal temperatures, even over a period of years. If the jump distance is about 2.5×10^{-10} m, to diffuse 1 millimetre into the steel would mean that a chromium atom had travelled a net distance of about four million jumps. Since the net distance travelled is proportional to the square root of the number of jumps, the poor little atom would need to make about 10^{13} jumps to travel one millimetre into the steel! Obviously considerable thermal energy is needed to persuade atoms to diffuse any significant distance in solids—even at 1 000 °C, it would take weeks rather than hours to diffuse the chromium layer into a steel bumper. Most applications of diffusion in technology require quite high temperatures, and because diffusion varies so rapidly with temperature the control mechanism must be quite sophisticated.

SAQ 27   On what factors do the rate of diffusion of, say, gold atoms in a piece of gold depend?

ANSWER   The important factors are temperature, the activation energy for diffusion and the atomic vibration frequency. The interatomic distance will also be important in determining the distance which an atom diffuses in a given time.

SAQ 28   What is the r.m.s. displacement of atoms which have made n diffusion jumps in a solid which has an interatomic distance a_0?

ANSWER $a_0 \sqrt{n}$.

8.6.3   Using diffusion in technology

Once the process of diffusion in a substance has been investigated, it sometimes becomes possible to use the effect to make materials more useful. We will look briefly at two examples of using diffusion to modify the properties of a material, making it more suitable for a particular application.

Case-hardening of steel is an important industrial process, used to manufacture parts which are both hard and tough. Conventional low-carbon steels are tough and springy, whereas high-carbon steels are hard and brittle. Many parts of a car engine, as well as exotic items like armour-plate, need to have a hard surface without being brittle. The solution is to have a low-carbon steel with a thin skin of high-carbon steel, which can be achieved by diffusing carbon into the surface layer of the steel. The process is known as carburizing. The simplest method involves packing a mixture of charcoal and some other substances, usually carbonates, around the steel part. The work is placed in a metal box, surrounded by the carburizing mixture, and heated to a temperature of about 900 °C. Carbon diffuses into the steel, forming a high-carbon layer. The thickness of the layer depends on the temperature and the time for which the job is heated, and tables of case-hardening depths in workshop manuals provide a good illustration of the rapid variation of diffusion rate with tempeature. Whereas it takes 25 hours to produce a case $1/8''$ thick at 870 °C, the same process takes only $11\frac{1}{2}$ hours at 960 °C. Carburizing can also be carried out by depositing carbon on the surface of the steel from a liquid or a gas. In all cases, the physical principle is the same: carbon atoms are added to the surface, and diffuse in to a carefully controlled depth.

case-hardening

It is not only the mechanical characteristics of a material which may be altered by diffusion. The electrical properties of semiconductors, such as silicon and germanium, are largely determined by the number of impurity atoms present and the nature of the impurities. The manufacture of transistors and integrated circuits with reproducible properties has been made possible by the crafty use of diffusion. Figure 22 shows a piece of a silicon chip, covered by an oxide layer. A window is etched into the oxide layer (2), a small amount of the desired impurity is deposited on the surface (3), and diffusion is used to create a layer which contains impurity atoms. This is known as a doped layer. The most usual impurities used are boron and phosphorus, each of which modifies the properties of the silicon in a characteristic way. Just as in carburizing, the impurity atoms are deposited on the surface (in this case by exposure to a gas) and driven into the solid to form a layer of known depth by heating.

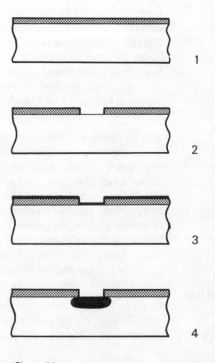

Figure 22   Steps in diffusing impurities into silicon.

The atoms become substitutional impurities, occupying lattice sites normally taken by silicon atoms, and diffuse by exchanging with vacancies. The whole process can be repeated to produce layers of doped regions, interacting to give the electrical properties required.

These two examples are very different. One is the diffusion of small carbon atoms through interstitials; the other is diffusion of impurity atoms which substitute for silicon atoms on normal lattice sites. One alters mechanical properties, the other varies electrical properties. Both rely on the basic principles of diffusion—the random walk of atoms jumping at a rate determined by temperature and the activation energy for the process—and illustrate how usefully basic knowledge can be applied to practical problems.

Unit·Titles ST 28—